THE CRAFT OF CHARACTER

HOW TO CREATE DEEP AND ENGAGING
CHARACTERS YOUR AUDIENCE WILL NEVER
FORGET

MARK BOUTROS

Edited by: Jasmin Naim

Cover by: Bobby Birchall, Bobby&Co

First Edition: February 2020

Print ISBN: 978-1-9162974-4-9

❀ Created with Vellum

CONTENTS

INTRODUCTION

C haracter is at the heart of every story. Of course, there are gripping plot points that stick in our minds, but that's because those moments happen to and through characters we are connected to. Those moments are actions taken or consequences suffered by characters, and we feel those moments because we are drawn to character.

There are great story concepts with strong hooks, but without a compelling character at the heart of a concept an idea becomes flat and forgettable. Characters are the experience and they give us something to love, hate and relate to. They make us want to keep watching and reading in the hope we get to see them finish their journey and get what they need or what we feel they deserve.

The aim of this book is to help you to develop characters that are lifelike, not just stock types we've met a thousand times before. Of course, stock types can be useful starting points, but you still have to make your characters come across as unique and banish clichés to avoid falling into stereotyping. A heavy reliance on stock types can steer us away from originality and encourage laziness in character development.

I've sat in many development meetings for new comedy

shows where people compare the characters in the new show to ones we've seen before. 'This is our Joey from *Friends*.' 'They can be our George from *Seinfeld*.' 'She's our Leslie from *Parks and Recreation*' and so on. That's normal as they do represent types, but if you're taking that approach and populating an idea with types, the key is to develop them from there. Problems occur when people think a close copy is good enough and then they don't take the time to get to the heart of a character, because they think the type is the heart.

It's no surprise that many ideas go from being bold and new to more of the same as fear grips the development process and dilutes character. Then those projects have little chance of being made unless there's a star name attached to add gravitas to a slender idea.

Rather than creating the new (insert name), create something new. Frasier Crane, Walter White, Arya Stark, Fleabag; they weren't the new someone else, they were new characters. Sadly, people now use them as frameworks to stick fresh characters into until the next hit comes along and the cycle repeats with a new template of characters.

In this book we'll discuss what character is and we'll touch upon story structure and dialogue because they flow through each other, but really this book is about understanding character so you can make yours as deep and emotionally engaging as possible. Everyone develops character differently, our brains naturally jump around and different triggers set us off in different directions, but I'll give you the essential questions you need to keep in your mind, whatever point you are at in your process.

Writers are always searching for a magic formula, but there isn't one. The path to better writing is to continually practice your craft and develop positive writing habits that inform your process. I will give you tools that help you to do this. The order I have written the chapters in is the order I find the most useful when developing character, but it's about creating processes that work for you, so once you've read it, shape what best fits your working methods.

I'll also look at common character mistakes and give you exercises to help you to understand your characters better.

Some of the exercises I set will annoy you and you'll be tempted to skip them thinking they don't matter, and that's entirely up to you, but I advise you to put the work in. How do you get to know people better? By spending time with them and moving from a shallow level of connection to a meaningful, deep one. It's the same with characters. By knowing your character deeply, you'll create someone engaging and multi-layered, and you'll make the writing process more fluid. You will find that plot comes out of your character instead of having to crowbar character into a plot. Development is about giving characters emotional depth and saving yourself time in the rewriting process.

I'll mostly use television programmes as references, but will also touch upon films, books, and I'll point out some of the differences between genres when it comes to characterisation.

Something I have struggled with in the past is the amount of references present in writing books, as I haven't read or seen most of them, so don't feel like you're less of a writer if you don't know the references I refer to. In the exercises I've given examples that should make up for any references that don't land.

A bit about me

I've worked as a writer and a producer for well over a decade on shows for the major UK broadcasters including the BBC, ITV, Channel 4, Sky One, Sky Arts, Disney and the Cartoon Network. I've written on *The Reluctant Landlord*, *The Amazing World of Gumball*, *The Dumping Ground*, and I co-wrote an episode called *The Greatest. Of All Time* about Muhammad Ali, which featured in season one of *Urban Myths* and was International Emmy nominated in 2018, and I won the silver in the PAGE International Screenwriting Awards in 2016.

One thing I've learned through my successes and failures is that problems start and end with character. Concerns arise such as, 'Why is the character doing this?' Or, 'Do I care about the character?' Or, 'I don't believe they'd do this.' Or, 'I've seen this before.'

In television, sometimes a producer will criticise a series pitch because they don't believe there is enough story to sustain multiple episodes. That doesn't mean you're missing plot, it means the character journey isn't engaging enough, because the character isn't developed well enough to carry a series.

I've made several mistakes on my writer's journey, but they've helped me to get to a point where I'm getting more jobs on existing shows and more of my original ideas optioned. I want to help you to avoid making the same mistakes I made, so you can improve your process sooner and know which pitfalls to watch out for.

For a full list of my credits you can visit www.mark-boutros.com/credits. I've had a scattered career from writing comedy, drama, fantasy, romance and crime, to teaching screenwriting and creating empathy in the Google Assistant, which is artificial intelligence but requires understanding of character nonetheless. All of my experiences have allowed me to develop skills in various areas but it always comes back to the same thing.

Character is the key to successful storytelling.

1

THE CORE OF CHARACTER

1.1. IT'S A STORY ABOUT SOMEONE WHO

If you break a story down it is essentially that. It's a story about someone who goes through something, who does something, who wants something and pursues it.

We all have different ways of finding character. Sometimes we create one out of something we've experienced. Sometimes someone exists fully formed who we think would be interesting to base a character around, perhaps a friend, a family member, or ourselves. Sometimes we construct someone to fit some major scene ideas we have in mind, or we have an incredibly catchy and unique concept we then need to populate with characters so we start from that point.

There are many ways to find inspiration, but however you work, it will always boil down to a story about someone who, whether it's in a film, audio drama, video game, book, or a TV show. It's our job as writers to take the ingredients that are becoming a character in our heads, and mould them into the completion of that sentence.

Some of us need to write experimental scenes that aren't part of any story to get to know characters, which I find an incredibly useful exercise. If you do this, make sure to have the

'It's a story about someone who...' in mind as you explore through writing.

Whether you're 20 pages into backstory development, have a word in mind that excites you, or a topic you are passionate about, all paths should lead to 'It's a story about someone who...'.

Example:

Breaking Bad is a story about someone who has inoperable cancer and turns to crime to provide for his family

Then developed out further:

Breaking Bad is a story about Walter White, a loyal father and chemistry teacher who is diagnosed with inoperable lung cancer. To guarantee his family's financial security he decides to produce crystal meth with his former student, Jesse Pinkman, but Walt soon realises this is something he's good at and he spirals into a life of crime, becoming his criminal alter ego

---

There are more twists and turns as the story progresses through the seasons, as well as a whole cast of characters around Walt who have their own journeys and their own perspectives and goals, but it's his story, and the other stories happen as a consequence of his decision to start making crystal meth.

As you can see, the first example starts simple. If you can say,

'It's a story about someone who...' then you have a story and a character, which together, convey that there is someone who does something. It also suggests that the thing the character does in relation to a trigger event is outside of their normal life. Walt enters a world he knows nothing about, and it is a world that poses great risk, because he is sick. He puts himself at risk in pursuit of a goal.

The second example adds layers to the character with some traits and a bit more drama. 'It's a story about someone who...' isn't a substitute for a great logline, but it's your jumping-off point to knowing you have a characterful story, that your story is about someone doing something and actively going after something. It's a step towards a great logline.

If you don't know what a logline is, one of the many definitions is: A one or two sentence summary of a story. However, that includes some key elements of the story:

1. Who is your main character?
2. What do they want?
3. Who/ what is in their way?
4. How do they overcome it?
5. Why does the protagonist (your hero) need to accomplish their goal?

Ultimately, a logline should give a quick sense of who the main character is and show them as relatable in some way. It should also highlight the event that changes the character's world and thrusts them into a story. This moment is often called the catalyst, inciting incident, or stranger comes to town, as it illustrates your character's everyday life being disturbed by something, be that an actual stranger, a letter or anything else out of the ordinary. The logline should also show us that your character faces difficult and important challenges.

Knowing the 'It's a story about someone who...' helps you to see your character's motivation. By knowing that the story is about a character who wants to provide for his family in desperate circumstances, we understand the reasons why Walt will do dark things, and we'll be engaged with him on this journey for that reason. The survival of loved ones and the need for money are strong motivators. They are primal needs many of the audience will have felt or at least will understand. Thankfully, most of us would not go to the extreme lengths Walter White did (I hope), nor do we have the skills to make the finest crystal meth in the land, but that's what makes his character stand out. We also recognise that Walt will face tough challenges as he enters a world outside of the society he has functioned within.

As the series progresses we learn that it becomes about Walt being good at this and being a winner, made clearer when we see that his former business partners are rich and that Walt is a bit of a loser. Now he's feeding his ego, and it has a big appetite. He also has felt the reality of his own mortality by being diagnosed with inoperable cancer, and with that comes a change of perspective that informs Walt's decisions. Think about it, if you were told you were going to die, how would that change your outlook on the world? Walt had no love for the world and a society that had clipped his wings. He was stuck, drowning in the mundane due to fear, so with a death sentence over his head he gained a sense of freedom and he decided to finally fly, albeit into the darkest place possible. By knowing 'It's a story about someone who...' the character can then develop further and you can add those extra layers.

What about ensemble shows and sitcoms?
They make it trickier to define an 'It's a story about someone who...', but it can become '...a story about a group of friends who...' or '...a story about a family that...' or in the case of *Game of Thrones*:

A story about the realm's noble families, battling for the Iron Throne

That runs over the entire span of the show, while within each episode there is a focus on specific characters driving their strand of a story, their own 'It's a story about someone who...'.

For example, in the first episode of *Game of Thrones*, one of the strands is:

A story about Ned Stark, who is asked to leave his home to rule alongside his friend, and king, Robert Baratheon, and for his daughter, Sansa, to marry the king's first son, Joffrey

The show is about multiple characters, all of whom want something and are on journeys of their own. Therefore the episodes will explore those characters and their motivations. They will all have an 'It's a story about someone who...' within the show's construction.

Another example of an episodic, ensemble story would be *Friends:*

A story about a group of twenty to thirty-something-year-old friends who live in Manhattan and help each other to navigate the pitfalls of love, family, work and friendship

Much like *Game of Thrones*, the 'It's a story about someone who...' sentence doesn't reveal much about one character nor is it that exciting, but we understand that at the heart of this show is a group of characters helping each other through life. As the concept develops out, we see that the individual episodes reveal more about the characters. Each has their moment to take centre stage and at different points there is romance, loss and other key, universally relatable events.

Let's look at season 4 episode 15, *The One With All The Rugby*. Within this episode there are three examples of 'It's a story about someone who.' A common formula for series that have self-contained episodes is to have an A, B and C story, each normally led by one of the characters (for more on A, B and C stories go to the Glossary). Here is an example from the aforementioned episode of *Friends*:

This is a story about Chandler who, desperate to be rid of Janice, his on-off girlfriend, lies about having to move to Yemen

This is also a story about Ross who, keen to impress his girlfriend Emily, plays rugby with her large friends, even though he has never played it

This is also a story about Monica, who is obsessed with finding out what a switch in her apartment does

You've got the makings of stories in all three statements that tell you something about each character. Chandler can't handle confrontation, Ross is desperate to impress even if it means hurting himself, and Monica is incredibly neurotic. The other main characters of the show will be involved in the other stories, and in other episodes will be the main focus. That's the beauty of a long-running comedy series, that you have a collection of well constructed characters to explore and you can shift focus over the seasons.

We'll focus on Chandler's story. There's a beginning, middle and end in there, and it's comedic, all from the perspective of character.

There is much more within the episode, but it already tells you plenty. The event that sets Chandler's story in motion is Janice coming back into his life while he is in a nail parlour with Rachel, but Chandler soon realises he shouldn't have gotten back with Janice. That leads him into having to take action, and Chandler is such a coward that rather than break up with Janice, he will lie about leaving the country to avoid her. However, his plan falls apart, because she loves him so much that she will spend every last minute she can with him, so the worst thing that can happen in this situation does, and he has to fly to Yemen.

What does it reveal about Chandler's character? He is a coward who hates confrontation. The right thing to do would be to tell Janice it's over, but he's scared of the repercussions. If you really think about it, it makes Chandler mean, yet we like him, because he's funny and useless and doesn't know what to do so he panics. His behaviour comes from fear rather than malice, plus Janice is annoying, which enables the writers to make Chandler behave like he does without making him too unlikeable. However, this is a horrible thing to do. He's leaving the country and leaving someone thinking there is hope. The right thing to do would be to dump her, and although that would hurt Janice and lead to Chandler getting told off, it would set Janice free and not have her pining for a love on the other side of the world, but it's in his character to behave as he did.

So from 'It's a story about someone who,' an entire, characterful story plays out in this episode. You can look at any sitcom over the years and find a story about someone dumping someone else. What makes a story feel new is the particular character going through it and how they uniquely approach that situation.

The concepts for *Game of Thrones* and *Friends* would be nothing without the characters behind the broader 'It's a story about someone who...'. So, even if you're starting with a wider concept ahead of character, put the time into making sure the characters behind the concept have their own stories within it to keep that concept from crumbling. Ross in *Friends*, for example, hops from marriage to marriage and also loses his mind during his journey, so as well as having an episodic 'It's a story about someone who...' for him, there is an overarching one, which is:

This is a story about Ross, whose childhood crush comes back into his life, and he gets her, loses her, and experiences heartache, a breakdown, and wrecks his way through relationships and marriages until he finally matures enough to be with her

You could even say *Friends* is a story about Ross and Rachel, who get together and break up, then go through life changing relationships and life milestones before realising they always needed each other. Within that basic concept of friends helping each other through pitfalls of life are stories relating to each character that keep the story itself going.

'It's a story about someone who...' can be traced back through time. For example:

> *Macbeth* is a story about a Scottish general who receives a prophecy from witches that he will one day become King of Scotland, and so, consumed by ambition and spurred on by his wife, he takes it by force

---

The reason you should always have 'It's a story about someone who...' in your mind is to place an early building block down that is designed to focus more on the character's beginnings in your story and illustrate that there is a journey to go on. Some call it the 'What if?' What if someone needed to dump someone but was too scared? What if all of the families in the realm fought to be the one true ruler? What if a terminally ill chemistry teacher became a drug dealer to provide for his family? Then you let your mind run and come up with how that character would behave. It allows for clarity, and clarity is one of the ways to engage with your audience, so they know who the character is early on, and the journey is defined. A great way to disengage someone from an experience is to confuse them. Confusion occurs when it isn't clear what goal a character is pursuing in a story (Chapter 1.2), and when their actions don't seem in line with their goal.

Whatever genre or medium you're writing, 'It's a story about someone who...' applies. So, when people ask the dreaded question, 'What are you writing at the moment?' Make it your task to be able to answer, 'I'm writing a story about someone who...', supplying sufficient detail to allow them to understand where you are going with your work. It allows you to focus on who you're telling a story about, and in ensemble stories you can reveal the concept then home in on the stories of your key characters.

Keep in mind that 'It's a story about someone who...' should primarily show there is a story, that someone is doing something because of something, then as you further define it you will see there is a goal that comes from relatable and understandable motivation.

EXERCISE 1

IT'S A STORY ABOUT SOMEONE WHO...

1a. Think of your favourite stories and break them down into the framework of 'It's a story about someone who...'. Try it with 5 - 10 examples.

If you include ensemble stories or ones that carry multiple character journeys, go layer by layer, starting with the broader concept, then focus on the character stories within a particular episode or over a series. Keep in mind the moment that propels your character into their story.

Here are some examples from films, TV shows and books to get you going:

Rocky is a story about a boxer with a loser's mentality who is offered the chance of a world title fight, but needs to see himself as a winner before he can step into the ring

---

Amelie is a story about a shy waitress who makes a surprising discovery and sees her life drastically changed for the better

———

Ex Machina is a story about a computer programmer who is chosen by his billionaire boss to participate in testing the human qualities of a prototype android

———

It's Always Sunny in Philadelphia is a story about a group of egocentric friends who own a failing pub and love nothing more than scheming and revelling in each other's misery

———

Lord of the Rings is a story about a young hobbit who inherits a ring that holds the secret to either the survival, or the enslavement, of the entire world

———

The Princess Bride is a story about a swash-buckling hero who teams up with a giant and a revenge-seeking swordsman in order to save the woman he loves from marrying an evil prince

———

1b. Come up with your own 'It's a story about someone who...'.

Remember to keep in mind that it's about someone who wants something, who does something and pursues something, and it includes that moment that takes your character out of their everyday.

I'll start you off by doing one of my own:

———

This is a story about a woman who has a heart attack and has to change the way she lives

———

Now I'll expand it out, thinking more about the character and adding a trait that fits to make her feel a bit more alive:

———

This is a story about a 35-year-old cynic who has to change the way she lives and her attitude, otherwise she won't make it to 40

———

And here's one for an ensemble show:

———

This is a story about tradespeople competing for work on the streets of the rich and famous, often using illegal techniques to get the work they're so desperate for

1.2. GOALS, DESIRES, AND THE NEED TO LEARN A LESSON

Whether you're creating a protagonist who is a lovely do-gooder or a ruthless murderer (more on anti-heroes in Chapter 2.3), it's about connection. Will an audience emotionally engage with and connect to your character? Obviously that is subjective, but there are techniques to increase the chances of engagement, and our job as writers is to make sure we give the audience every chance to want to spend time with our characters.

Give your character a clear goal
One of those techniques is to give your character a clear goal. By understanding what a character is pursuing, an audience then understands what motivates your character's behaviour. Everything your character does should be informed by what they want.

It is far more interesting to know what someone wants and to watch them pursue it than to question why they're doing things the entire time. There's a fine line between intrigue and confusion, and motivation should never be confusing. If we don't know why someone is doing something, then we will search for it, and that creates distance rather than connection, because if we don't know why someone is doing something, then why should we care that they're doing it?

Fuel the goal with a deeper emotional desire

As well as making your character's goal clear, the desire behind the goal needs to have emotional importance for them and be strong enough that your character makes difficult decisions and takes risks. The desire needs to be universally relatable or understandable to an audience.

Take Walter White, for example. In the early stages of *Breaking Bad*, his goal is to make money to leave his family financially secure before he dies, because he has a desire to be a good husband and father, looking out for his family and putting them first. So his emotional, internal desire behind his external goal, comes from a relatable and understandable place that makes him easy to connect with. Family survival and financial security are big motivators and big fears, and he places himself in a world full of risk in order to get those things. If he fails he will either go to jail, be murdered by drug dealers, or die from cancer with his family being no better off as a result of his actions (more on stakes in Chapter 1.3).

An emotional, universally relatable and understandable desire is essential to building connection between your protagonist and the audience. Goals and desires are also necessary in other characters. Villains are more interesting when their villainy comes from real motivation. Nobody wants to take over the world for the sake of it, and being bad just for the sake of being bad makes villains flat. Motivate them to breathe life into them.

Desires tend to come from something primal that we can identify with, such as the desire to feel love, to have enough money, to have an identity and feel connected, to feel safe, or to protect or have a family. They tap into fears.

In simpler terms, your character needs to pursue an external goal as it is what drives the story, and the emotional desire behind the goal informs that pursuit and motivates your character to make difficult decisions. Without an emotional desire informing the goal, the goal is worthless.

Make your protagonist learn something

Another technique to increase engagement across your protagonist's journey is for us as writers to understand what they need to learn. The lesson is often learned towards the end of your story. It's what your protagonist discovers about themselves in order to overcome their final confrontation. It shows change.

It is easier to see the lesson in action across films and books as they are often contained within a single story, as opposed to multiple episodes. For example, in *500 Days of Summer*, Tom wants his ex, Summer, back, because he believes she is his true love and that true love is the only thing that will make him happy. However, by going on the journey he does, he learns true happiness lies within the self, and that he needs to look inwards. It gives him hope for a future and the film ends with him going for a job he wants and meeting a girl symbolically named Autumn.

The lesson is often what your character emotionally needs to understand in order to find the fulfilment that the external goal is only masking. For Tom to find true love, he needs to stop pinning his hopes on Summer who wasn't as perfect as he remembers, and only by nurturing himself will he find the complete package of happiness.

The lesson is hard to find, because it comes so late in the story, but as a writer you can find this by asking that question about your character's goal. What emotional issue is the goal they're pursuing masking? What flaw does it come from? (More on flaws in Chapter 1.4).

The key thing to remember is that your character's behaviour is informed by the goal they pursue and the emotional desire it comes from, so they won't be consciously acting with the intention of learning a lesson. The idea is that they don't even know what they need to learn. That comes out through the journey and the highs and lows, but you should know it when writing so you know where your character ends up. It's useless when facing a blank page, but it is where the road leads.

Let's look at Walter White's lesson. I've mentioned his goal being to make money to leave his family financially secure before he dies, because he has a desire to be a good father and husband, looking out for his family and putting them first. However, he needs to learn that being a good father and husband is being present rather than becoming a drug lord. His love is more important to them than his money, but he doesn't learn this lesson. What he learns is that he has been living the wrong life for too long, and over the course of the story he chooses to commit to a life of crime and darkness to feed his ego. He is corrupted by pride and greed, and it leads to his death. Not all emotional lessons are ones that lead the character to a positive end, but there is a still a change marked by a character learning something.

Here are clearer definitions of goals, desires, and lessons as you flesh something out:

The goal is what your character actively seeks out. For example:

- A detective wants to <u>find her missing son</u>...
- A donkey wants to be <u>accepted into the circus</u>...

- A runner wants to <u>win a big race</u>...

Desires are the motivation behind the goal, and must be emotionally significant, relatable, with clear positive and negative outcomes. For example:

- A detective wants to <u>find her missing son</u>, because <u>she desires closure</u>... (She hopes it will be positive and that she will find him, but there is the risk it is negative and he is confirmed dead. Loss, fear, family and wanting to protect those we love is relatable).
- A donkey wants to be <u>accepted into the circus</u>, because <u>they desire love and adoration</u>... (They hope it will be positive and they will be loved, but there is a negative risk of rejection. Desiring identity and acceptance is relatable).
- A runner wants to <u>win a big race</u>, because <u>she desires the approval of her coach</u>... (She hopes it will be positive and she will have her coach's approval and value herself, but there is a negative risk of failure and never being accepted. Desiring approval and lacking a sense of self-worth are both relatable)

Lessons are more abstract and relate to a deeper emotional need that the character must discover on their journey. For example:

- A detective wants to <u>find her missing son</u>, because <u>she desires closure.</u> However, the detective needs to accept her son is gone and <u>learn to forgive herself.</u>

- A donkey wants to be <u>accepted into the circus,</u> because <u>they desire love and adoration.</u> However, the donkey needs to <u>learn to love themselves before they seek the love of others.</u>
- A runner wants to <u>win a big race,</u> because <u>she desires the approval of her coach.</u> However, she needs to <u>learn to be her own person, and not the person her coach wants her to be.</u>

Often your character will think that by achieving their goal, that they will fulfil their deeper emotional desire, but the real lesson tends to be buried underneath it all, so that the character is blind to it, but the journey progression and obstacles they face (more on obstacles in Chapter 2.2) are what open their eyes.

If there is no desire, no motive behind every action, there is no journey. All the things your character does should be with their goal in mind.

Goals, desires, and lessons come back to the character being the experience. Watching them pursue something, we want to understand the reason why they are pursuing it and feel like we can relate to the desire behind it. When we think about plot, it needs to run through the character and come from their emotional state, and that needs to be a consequence of what they are pursuing. All the action in *Taken* comes from Liam Neeson wanting to find his daughter, because he desires to protect her and will be devastated if he can't and his family will be broken. This leads to lots of people getting punched and things being blown up.

The goal, desire, and lesson are core aspects of making a character engaging. Without them, you have a shell, doing things for no particular reason, and that is neither engaging nor entertaining.

You don't always need to have your character explicitly state their goal and desire, as audiences feel a sense of achievement and reward when they can piece things together themselves. However, you still need to make goals and desires clear early on, and that's where your craft comes into it.

For example, if a character says, 'I am so poor, I wish I had money, but nobody will give me a job and my mum is sick', it tells us what we need to know but is boring and spoon feeds the audience. It is far more engaging for to see the character get up in their run down home, go to the kitchen and get out two bowls, open the empty fridge, open a cupboard and take out an old cereal box that only contains enough for one, and then take that one bowl of dry cereal to their mum who is bedridden so she can eat, and then go and look for jobs and get rejected. It allows the audience to create the image, thus engaging their brain. At this point we don't know what the lesson is, but maybe over the story it is that this character needs to learn to accept that they can't care for their mother anymore and they need help, but that doesn't mean they're a bad child, because their love is enough. This could be a story about self-acceptance and understanding what love is.

There's a popular saying, 'show don't tell.' This is an example where you show a character struggling, instead of having them say how much they're struggling. It also clearly defines a goal, a desire, and suggests a lesson for me to work with but no more than that. Clarity is there through action.

You must know the emotional desire behind a goal when writing because the question you always have to be able to answer while writing is, 'Why is my character doing this?' It makes it easier to understand a character's behaviour, and in turn makes them more engaging. This doesn't only apply to protagonists, but all characters. Take Mike in *Breaking Bad*. He is a corrupt police officer turned right-hand man to Gustavo, a mob boss. He is brilliant at operating on both sides of the law.

Why does he do it? Later in his story we learn that it's about more than making money. It's about making money to keep in an account in his granddaughter's name. He has an emotional drive and a human connection. His desire is primal, looking out for family in the way he best knows how. Another reason for him doing what he does is because his son was also a policeman who was killed by other corrupt officers, and it shaped his worldview and humanity.

Always have 'why?' in the back of your mind. 'Why does my character want this?' 'Why haven't they given up yet?' 'Why aren't they fulfilled without this?' 'Why would they put themselves at risk for this thing?' 'Why don't they stop what they're doing now that they seemingly have enough?'

Behind all the goals and desires and stories about people who, is a why. Everything in this book will always link back to that. Think about your own life, why do you work where you work? Why do you like one person and not another? Why are you scared of what you're scared of? Why do you want to change the thing about yourself that you want to change? There is a reason behind every action and decision. Sometimes choices are imposed on you by circumstance and external factors, but often your decisions come from somewhere else. Nothing is ever meaningless. It's the same with character and we have to mine to get beneath the surface, bring up the gold and create real people. A great way to develop your characters is to analyse yourself and ask yourself why you do the things you do.

An example of a goal, desire, and lesson in action comes from a BBC children's show called *The Dumping Ground*. This is a series about children in a care home, and each episode is a complete story. In one episode a character called Floss gives one of the carers tips on which children are misbehaving, because she wants to get into his good books by making everyone else look worse. She thinks this will get her the trumpet lessons she wants. That's her goal, trumpet lessons, and it's something external, not an emotion. This is her clearly defined goal, and on the surface she wants the lessons because she is rubbish at the trumpet.

Her obstacle to getting the lessons is that there isn't enough money to give everyone what they want. So her plan is to make herself look good by making everyone else look bad, which she does by getting them into trouble. She succeeds. Her friends look bad and she is offered the lessons. But in succeeding, she and her close friend, Alex, fall out because he learns of her underhand methods. Floss explains that she made everyone else look bad because she wants the trumpet lessons so she can be good at something, because she feels like she has nothing that makes her stand out.

That is the emotional desire behind it all, to stand out, to shape her identity, which is expressed via her pursuit of the goal throughout the episode. However, in the end, having succeeded in achieving her goal she declines the trumpet lessons, comes clean to her carer and repairs her friendship, because she learns a valuable lesson, which is that she can feel part of the house through friendship.

So why does she want trumpet lessons? To get better at playing the trumpet.

Why? Because she desires to be good at something, to stand out and to forge her identity in a house of many children where she doesn't always fit in. She feels disconnected.

What is her emotional lesson? That her friend accepting her as she is, is enough. By getting what she thinks will fulfil her desire, she loses Alex's friendship and realises that is what matters, so she takes steps to repair it, because deep down, friendship satisfies her desire.

Motivation comes from desire.

I like to think of the goal as the brain, and the desire as the heart, and the lesson as the soul. These are integral to your character existing at all.

If you don't know your character's goal and desire, don't start writing the script or manuscript. That's where the 'It's a story about someone who...' helps. Knowing who it's about and what they're doing helps you to shape these clearer definitions and motivations and get to those answers. These are fundamentals of character. A lot of character develops through writing and getting to know them through bringing them to life and having them interact, but a goal and desire makes them exist in the first place. If you jump into a draft without knowing them then you will find the redrafting process far more brutal.

Give your characters a brain, heart, and soul before you send them on a journey. Some writers like to do what is known as a vomit draft where you freely write whatever is inside and let it spill onto the page to get the story out of you. It's a disgusting image but it explains it well. However, that draft is at least partially informed by the core of character. You need something inside to vomit onto the page.

Goals and desires feed motivation, and a lesson learned shows change. With those three things you're on your way to a great character and story.

People often email me asking how to create compelling characters, because they have created a cool backstory, but have not developed the character any further. This means that there is no story going forwards. So, if you're a writer who likes to go heavy on backstory first, then have in mind that your character has to want something for backstory elements to become relevant to a story. Backstory is great for informing the 'why', so it's up to you to keep in mind that through all the backstory development, you need to be looking for what desire propels a character into a story in pursuit of a goal. Backstory is meaningless if there is no onward journey for your character. Story doesn't begin until your character has a goal.

When Neil Webster and I co-wrote the *Urban Myth* about Muhammad Ali, we were fortunate in that it was based on an existing news article and video, and that Ali is such a well-known character with mannerisms and a backstory familiar to many people. However, we still had to establish his goal, desire, and the lesson he had to learn to succeed. That came from research and character development.

The story is about Muhammad Ali trying to save a man from committing suicide. His goal is to save a man from killing himself, but we had to find a deep desire. Our research (more on research tips in Chapter 2.6) uncovered that merely weeks before this incident, Ali had lost his penultimate fight and people were telling him to quit. It was also his birthday only a few days prior to the event. So, we had a character facing his own mortality in and out of the ring, now in a situation involving life and death.

In terms of the dynamic, we had Muhammad Ali, the world's greatest, and Joe, the suicidal man who thinks he's the world's worst. They each had a perspective and a self-assigned position in this story world that placed them at opposite ends of the spectrum. That was a great starting point.

So Ali's goal is to save Joe. He believes by saving Joe he will prove to the world and himself that he is still 'the champ.' There are news crews and a crowd watching, adding a layer that this is another event people are here to see Muhammad Ali for. However, the lesson he needs to learn is to be Ali the vulnerable human.

Ali's attempts to succeed in his goal come from behaving like Ali 'the champ', because he believes the rhyming and the confidence will help him to save Joe, and he believes the world wants him to always be 'the champ'. However, he only succeeds when he reconciles his flaw (more on flaws in Chapter 1.4) and learns his real lesson, which is that it's okay to be Ali the human, who is just as lost as Joe. By confronting this fact about himself, and showing a vulnerability that brings him down from his godly pedestal, he connects with Joe on a human level, and succeeds.

He fulfils his desire to be the champ, but it's a different kind of champ, a champ outside the ring who can overcome different kinds of challenges.

The goal and desire are always easier to find than the lesson, but if you dig in and ask why your character wants the thing they want and attack that desire, you start to unearth deeper emotional reasons that make for an entertaining and engaging journey. The question 'why?' is your best friend at getting out of trouble and developing more compelling characters. However, if audiences are asking 'why?' it becomes your worst enemy.

So, in summary, whatever your development process, keep in mind that, for your character to have emotional depth and to increase audience connection:

- They need to want something and to pursue it. Your main character's goal drives the story, and that goal needs to be clear. There is no bigger killer of engagement than confusion.
- The goal should be something meaningful to them, and represent a great challenge.
- They must have an emotional desire connected to the goal and hope to satisfy it through succeeding. It should be universally relatable or understandable.
- A goal is worthless if it doesn't carry emotional significance.
- There needs to be something even deeper at play that they don't know yet, a lesson they must learn that is the true illustration of success in this story. If they get what they want without learning anything about themselves, their lives will likely remain unchanged, but if they learn that lesson about themselves, their journey will be transformative and positive.

Do all the characters in your story have to have goals, desires and learn lessons?

I believe every character should have a goal and desire. It enriches the world you're creating and enlivens interactions. If my character, Julie, has a job interview and goes in, and the interviewer has no goal in that scene, it is very one-sided and boring. However, if the interviewer wants to make it quick to get lunch, then it creates more panic in Julie and is in opposition to what she wants, and complicates her achieving her goal. It adds conflict and destabilises her. However, make sure you know why minor characters want what they want as well.

Your protagonist is the one who must learn an emotional lesson. In a film or book, that is the transformative journey. In a serial drama like *Breaking Bad*, it also applies, but doesn't happen in every episode. It is an evolution of character across multiple episodes and seasons. In episodic TV, like *The Dumping Ground*, where every episode is self-contained, the main character needs to have that transformative journey within the episode. In sitcom, it isn't necessary, as the characters aren't meant to learn, and even if they do, they reset by the next episode.

What about in different genres?

In slasher and many horror films a lesson is less apparent, as most of the time we're just waiting for a character to die, and in action films a protagonist may not learn anything deeply meaningful about themselves. However, in films where a character doesn't learn something emotional, they still tend to learn something in order to succeed. Take *Jaws,* for example, Brody doesn't learn anything deeply emotional. He has to overcome his fear of water, but the main thing he learns is how to overcome the shark. Through their battle, he realises the strategy of an expert fisherman and someone who studies sea life isn't working, and seemingly on the brink of death, he uses a canister and shoots it to blow the shark up.

However, we are looking at constructing compelling characters in 2020 onwards, and for me, the most memorable are the ones who have a lesson to learn, and their decision to learn it or ignore it reveals something about character and makes them memorable. Ideally, even in an action film or horror your character will learn something about themselves that informs how they overcome their greatest challenge.

EXERCISE 2

GOALS, DESIRES AND LESSONS

2a. What is your character's goal?

A goal can also be to lose something. Someone may want to dump someone, get rid of an item that is dangerous, but it follows the same principles and comes down to why and what their desire represents.

I'll continue my example:
My character, Julie, wants to get better. That is her goal. It's not an item but it is an attainable goal, achieved either by a doctor saying, 'Your health is much better', or her feeling better and us realising she has changed. That is her story goal. If she decides to confront her bossy mother, or give up drinking, it's because she believes they are steps towards her goal.

———

2b. What deep emotional desire will your character succeeding fulfil?

Example:

Julie's desire is to not feel broken and to feel accepted in the world. By getting better she will no longer feel weak or pathetic or disconnected. Being unwell makes her feel inferior, so her emotional desire is to feel 'fixed'.

The positive outcome is that she succeeds and feels whole, but the negative is she doesn't and is miserable and might have another heart attack.

2c. What lesson does your character need to learn to succeed?

Example:

Julie needs to learn to be vulnerable. To achieve this, she needs to open herself up to the world.

She wants to get better, but wants to do it by being the same as she's always been, with her guard up and without letting the world in. She sees the world as an enemy and is always on the defensive. She only sees the misery and the dark and the negative, so her soul is her need to let love in and love herself. Until she can reconcile her head, heart, and soul, she will struggle, so her attempts to get what she wants will be hindered by her inability to do what she needs until she grows throughout her journey. She needs to realise that the only way to let love in is to open herself up to the world and risk hurt and vulnerability. It's a two-way process for her.

So if this is a comedy series, each episode, she will aim to tackle her problem, and change will be teased with little moments, but she will never truly succeed until towards the end of the final episode when she fully embraces vulnerability.

Julie's goal. Her head: To get better and avoid another heart attack.

Julie's desire. Her heart: To be happy and not feel broken (the positive is that she succeeds and feels whole, but the negative is she doesn't and is miserable and might have another heart attack).

Julie's lesson. Her soul: To learn that she needs to show vulnerability.

After suffering a heart attack, Julie wants to address the problems in her life, because she desires to feel part of the world. However, she needs to learn to be vulnerable, to let people get close to her, and to stop blaming her problems on others, otherwise she will repeat the same mistakes.

Extra task

Introspection is crucial in character development, so think of three times you've wanted something, and why you wanted it, but get deep with the analysis and keep asking why.

For example, someone wants to have lunch with their ex.

Why? To say the things they never got to say.

Why do they desire to say the things they never got to say? Because they think it will help them to move on and they feel like they never got to say their piece.

Why is that important to them? Because they've had several failed relationships and always bring it back to that one.

Keep going with it until it starts to unearth deeper motivation that you can attribute to a deep lesson. Through further questions, we may learn the person in the above example is blaming their ex when the real problem is something within they haven't reconciled. Everything comes from a deep motive.

Motivation is crucial in creating understanding and informs

behaviour. The deeper you go, the more unique and engaging your character becomes.

Always dig deeper.

1.3. RAISE THE STAKES

A s well as goals, desires and lessons, there needs to be a threat to your character on their journey. What happens if they don't get what they want? The consequence of failure needs to be high, even in a comedy, as that's what makes us care. If a character goes through something and it doesn't matter whether they succeed or fail, then what is there to become emotionally invested in? The audience needs to understand the joy and pain that faces your character in order to feel the journey. The more your character stands to lose, the higher the highs, the lower the lows, and the more engaged we are.

For Muhammad Ali in our *Urban Myth*, failure meant the death of Joe, with the eyes of the world watching. On a personal level this would be another public failure after Ali's previous boxing match, and the power he believes he has would dwindle further. As well as the death of Joe, it would be the death of the champ. Ali would have lost both a fight in the ring and a fight outside the ring within a short amount of time. Imagine having the death of someone on your conscience. You set out to save someone, but the opposite happened. That would be horrific, and as writers, it is our job to bring our characters face to face with the ultimate consequence and tease that it could happen. It is in that moment of true fear that true character is often revealed.

Stakes are obvious to see in stories like *Avengers: Infinity War*, and *The Lord of the Rings*. Failure will mean death to all and the world in misery. However, in stories that aren't about evil consuming everything, the consequences don't have to be that the world will crumble, but they should involve your character's world crumbling, both internally and externally. The higher the stakes are for your character, the scarier it is for them, the more vulnerable they are and the more we can connect with them. Vulnerability strikes a chord in us, because we've all been vulnerable.

Internally, Muhammad Ali would have failed and will be feeling his mortality and may never forgive himself.

Externally, the world would see him as a failure and Ali the star would fade further.

Think of someone in your friendship group, or someone you've met whom you have no connection to outside of co-existing in the same social circle, writing group or workplace. Have you ever had a conversation with them in which they expressed a hint of vulnerability? How did that make you feel? For me, I have a friend from school who has the cold exterior of a government agent. We have nothing in common, but we were sitting next to each other at a birthday party, when later in the evening he opened up about his struggles to have kids, and we connected, because this was someone telling me he was in pain because he couldn't get what he wanted, and that all he ever wanted was a child, so at stake was something deeply personal to the world he existed in and wanted to create. He always wanted to live in a world where he was a father.

It's human nature to try to understand, and in a selfish way to place ourselves in situations to form that understanding, and from the moment he said that a child was all he ever wanted, I was engaged in his story. I hoped he would get what he wanted, and from time to time I checked in with him to find out how it was going and he would message me with progress, the highs and the lows. There are stories all around us, and people are going through journeys with things at stake to their world every day, and the things we have in common with people, whoever they are, are goals, desires, and fears. Whatever way those things present themselves, they allow us to understand.

Stakes raise the drama, and all stories are dramatic journeys. If my friend couldn't have a child but didn't care because he'd get a cat instead, then there is nothing at stake. But if his problem created tension in his marriage or pushed him into a dark hole of misery, then there are stakes and things he's fighting for. When it comes to character, the bigger and more threatening stakes are to your character's world, the better. The way characters react to adversity reveals a lot about them, so if there is no adversity or threat, we'll learn nothing about them and the journey won't feel worth it.

Stakes don't need to threaten the world, but they need to threaten your character's world, both internally and externally

Think of Marlin in *Finding Nemo*, who will be alone forever if he doesn't find his son, Nemo. The wider world will be fine, but his world will be devastated, and this is made more powerful because in the past, Marlin also lost the love of his life, Coral. It makes the stakes even higher because it ramps up the pain. That is an added layer of great suffering and generates sympathy from the audience.

Stakes make us connect to character, because we know loss

hurts, especially if we know your character has felt a deep loss before and it may have led to them having a particular worldview. For example, in *Finding Nemo*, the opening scene shows Marlin and Coral deeply in love, having just moved to a new home, and they're excited that they will soon have children. Then a barracuda eats Coral. In that opening sequence we see great love turn into great loss, and the next scene shows Marlin's worldview has been shaped by it. When he sends Nemo off to school he tells him to repeat what Marlin has told him about the ocean, which is that the ocean is not safe. Marlin's worldview comes from trauma and a past, deeply negative experience.

Everyone has experienced some kind of loss or at least fears loss, so if we can relate to someone, seeing them threatened compels us to stay locked in. Stakes make characters vulnerable, and vulnerability is a door to understanding and empathy.

So when it comes to stakes:

- There needs to be a real danger that your character fails.
- It needs to hang over their every move and grow more and more ominous.
- The consequence of that failure also needs to be destructive to your character's internal and external world.
- They need to come face to face with their worst fear, as how they react reveals so much about them. None of us wants to come face to face with our worst fear, so seeing it happen to someone else is gripping.

EXERCISE 3

RISING STAKES

3. What is at stake for your character?

Think about the internal and external stakes to your character and why the audience will care about this. Ask yourself what makes the stakes relatable. And think about what the worst thing that can happen to your character is in the event that they don't get what they want.

Example:

At stake is Julie's happiness and health. Two quite big things. And when people connect with her they'll want her to be happy and healthy, so I need to show that struggle. Her failure would be failing to open up her heart. It would be a metaphorical death and the knife will sink in and she will be stuck in a negative loop and probably have another heart attack, or live miserably until she dies as the world moves on around her. A life full of potential wasted, due to fear. The stakes are relatable as people can understand what it is like to feel disconnected, disinterested, and to carry the fear that they won't live a life that allows them to be happy.

Externally at stake - Her health (physical, and in some ways emotional).

Internally at stake - Her happiness and her sense of connection to the world (emotional).

Now you've done that, your character should have a brain, heart, soul, and a gun pointed at them.

1.4. CHARACTER FLAWS

W hen trying to sell an idea, if it isn't clear, you will likely get asked, 'What is your protagonist's flaw?'

Every protagonist needs a flaw, otherwise what are they doing in your story? Imagine a flawless person. Could you relate to someone with zero flaws? Would you want to watch a story or read a book about someone with no flaw? Flaws allow us to connect with everyone from the hero to the villain.

A flaw is an imperfection, a bias or a limitation of some kind. It is a deficiency in an otherwise functioning character, or a blind spot. If the goal is the brain, the desire the heart, and the lesson to be learned the soul, then the flaw is a wound on that soul that shapes your character's worldview, and it is often based on a past trauma. The flaw is what stops them learning their lesson, and either they overcome that flaw and heal their soul, or they fail and the wound becomes incurable. A flaw is an obstacle to emotional growth. It creates internal conflict while they pursue their external goal.

Character flaws can range from anything like a lust for power to prioritising career advancement over significant others, or jealousy. The key to any flaw is the why behind it. Why does

Marlin in *Finding Nemo* believe the ocean is dangerous and want nothing to do with it? Because he lost the love of his life to a barracuda. To him the wider ocean represents loss and taps into his fears, and that fear informs his beliefs.

Why would someone be jealous? Perhaps they were cheated on, and now they are eternally suspicious in relationships and have a need for control.

It is also important to know the difference between a flaw and a negative personality trait (more on traits in Chapter 2.4), as the two are often blurred.

A flaw has a stronger connection to the problem the character faces than a negative personality trait. A flaw causes real trouble and is a deep and unresolved emotional issue, often linked to the past, whereas something like being clumsy is a negative trait with no real roots in anything deeply emotional or unresolved, unless you're writing a comedy and you engineer a daft way to link clumsiness to a deeper trauma.

The flaw connects to backstory. If I grew up in poverty and saw it rip my parents' marriage apart, perhaps I now have a deep-rooted belief that only money can make me happy, and therefore I'm stingy and don't share. That is a flaw, because my behaviour towards others comes from a belief based on past trauma. If my goal is then to find love, but I only date rich people and ignore my colleague who is amazing but poor because I measure happiness and worth in monetary terms, then I need to overcome the belief/ flaw, which is based on my past experience in order to grow as a person and to be open to the possibility of real love. I need to understand that happiness is spiritual not financial. If I can't do that then I will end up with someone I shouldn't be with and will maintain my view that money is the primary factor in happiness, so I won't even see that I shouldn't be with my partner, and will probably be miserable but accepting of that misery.

Flaws leave room for growth and change, and we connect with flaws and can relate to them. Without a flaw, a character has nowhere to go. Flaws need to feel genuine too, and the best ones often come from fear, because people do whatever they can to avoid the thing they fear, because there is a reason for fear; it often comes from experience. Again, it comes down to the why. Why is my character scared to get close to people? Why is my character scared of being rejected? Why does my character remain closed off? If a character has been left at the altar in the past, perhaps they have a fear of marriage or commitment.

Often the reason a character comes across as weak or under-developed is because they lack a flaw, or possess one that feels like an afterthought. Flaws allow the character arc to be trans-formative, to move from the negative into the positive, or even from positive to negative. In the context of television drama, a character starts out as someone who gradually transforms into a different person based on their experiences over a series. Take Walter White in *Breaking Bad*, who over five seasons goes from down-and-out chemistry teacher to meth kingpin, because his flaw, his wounded pride and ego, pulls him deeper into the darkness.

When trying to sell a series it is the norm to write a pilot script and a series outline, and in that outline you need to state the character arc, so the potential buyer knows the journey your character will go on.

A character's flaw should relate to the lesson.

Let's look at the Chandler example again from *Friends*. He wants to dump Janice, but he's terrified, because he's done this before. His flaw is fearing confrontation, because it requires honesty, and that leads him to lie and go to Yemen. To tell her the truth would mean acknowledging his own deficiency when it comes to love and loving, and perhaps then having to acknowledge where that comes from, which is his parents. In another episode his mum kisses Ross, and we learn that his dad is a drag artist, so his issues with commitment could stem from his past, the relationship between his parents and their behaviour. So he goes to great lengths to avoid dumping Janice outright, and the result is that he goes to Yemen.

It's worth noting in traditional sitcom that the characters aren't meant to overcome their flaws or regularly learn lessons, as a lot of their conflicts come from those flaws. Think of David Brent in *The Office*, who will never stop thinking he is hilarious, and his brand of comedy is what gets him into so much trouble and is cringe worthy. Larry David in *Curb Your Enthusiasm* will forever be neurotic and unwilling to compromise and the comedy comes from that. Sitcom characters might acknowledge flaws at the end of an episode after they've lost the battle, but in the next episode it's right back to zero, so they never learn anything significant enough to change, because those same flaws need to drive them into a new story in the following episode.

Think back to our donkey that wants to join the circus because it desires love (Chapter 1.2). Its flaw could be that it places its sense of self in the perception of others, so it always tries to please and acts in ways to impress others. It needs to learn to love itself and be itself before it can be loved by anyone else, so the flaw links to the lesson to be learned.

Let's study *Jaws*. Chief Brody's flaw is that he is scared of the water because of a near-drowning experience as a child. It's simple - past trauma preventing present goal from being accomplished. After a shark attack, he hopes that putting signs on the beach to deter people will mean his job is done, but when the greedy mayor who only cares about tourism demands the signs come down and allows the shark to claim more lives, Brody's son is nearly killed. At that point, Brody knows that he has to confront his flaw in order to defend his family and the future of the town of Amity, which relies on tourism, so he gets on a boat with two other flawed characters and battles the shark.

It's easy to slap a flaw onto your character like an accessory from a long list, but it will stick out as forced unless you choose carefully and have a real reason why you're choosing that particular flaw and weaving it into your character's existence. To get a genuine, characterful flaw, you need to delve deeper into your character, and a handy way is to relate it to your 'It's a story about someone who...' By knowing *Jaws* is a story about Chief Brody, who has to confront a shark that is terrorising his town, you can then think, what about him makes this more complicated? What adds more conflict? A fear of water. Not only is he going into enemy territory, he's terrified of it, and him putting himself in a position of fear to protect others makes him more likeable and engaging and the stakes are even higher.

In *Top Boy* series 3, Dushane's flaw is his moral compass. The thing that is good and that makes us connect with him is the thing that holds him back from achieving his goal, which is to be the top boy in his area. He exists in a dark world, and later in the series we see him accept that. He is initially back in London from Jamaica to make money for a drug lord who will kill him and his disabled cousin if he doesn't cooperate. But once Dushane's cousin dies, it shows Dushane that morality means nothing and in a way, the death frees him from it. When on the brink of the final showdown with his ruthless rival, Jamie, Dushane tells his long-time friend and business partner, Sully, that this is all they can ever be. There is no other life or career choice. They are drug dealers, and the death of his cousin hammered that home. In that moment, Dushane realises that to be the top drug dealer, the one people respect, fear and do business with, and to not die (high stakes), he has to abandon both his moral code and street code, so he gets the police involved in his war and they arrest Jamie.

Dushane has won, but at what cost? He has changed from

someone who wants to survive within the rules of the world he knows where there are street values, to someone who is willing to break the rules to get what he wants.

Sully even tells him that although they didn't lose the war, they didn't win it either. The series is an example of someone wanting something to fulfil a desire, and learning a lesson that allows him to overcome a flaw to get what he wants in the face of dire consequences. All the characters in the series have a goal, desire and a flaw, and when writing we should always aim to give all of our characters that much depth. Everyone needs to feel real, even if they don't all overcome their flaws.

Of course, if you look through the history of film, books and television you will find several examples of characters who don't overcome flaws, but think about your favourite stories. How many contain rounded and well-developed characters? Deep and flawed characters enhance an entertainment experience and show whomever you're trying to sell your work to that you have a strong understanding of your craft.

For a meaningful flaw that makes your character stand out, think about it in terms of:

- What wound does it come from?
- How does their flaw relate to their goal and shape their worldview?
- How does their flaw prevent them getting what they want?
- Do they initially view their flaw as a strength?
- What would need to happen for them to face their flaw?

Protagonists and even antagonists with flaws are more interesting and three-dimensional. If someone is perfect they are boring. They have nothing that needs solving. Likewise, someone with too many flaws we may find distasteful and repellent. Some people say a flaw is a tool, but I would argue it is an essential part of creating an engaging character. What's the point in a story if a character isn't trying to overcome something external and internal? Life is about making sense of the world and ourselves, because deep down we are all flawed. Make your characters lifelike by giving them flaws.

EXERCISE 4

FINDING THE FLAW

4a. Answer some questions.

To understand character, try to understand yourself. This exercise may feel like therapy, but it shows the complexity of character. Answer the following questions:

1. What is my happiest memory and why?
2. What is my saddest memory and why?
3. When have I felt genuine pride and why?
4. When have I felt genuine shame and why?
5. When have I been most scared and why?
6. When was the first time I thought I understood love and why?
7. To me, what is the meaning of life and why?
8. What about me is stopping me getting what I want and why?
9. What belief do I have that regularly creates conflict and where does it come from?
10. When was a time I was emotionally hurt?

Now think about all of those moments and write down how a

negative one may have shaped a particular worldview you have. Has one of those events influenced how you behave day to day?

4b. Answer the same questions about your character and write an exploratory scene for each.

1. What is their happiest memory and why?
2. What is their saddest memory and why?
3. When have they felt genuine pride and why?
4. When have they felt genuine shame and why?
5. When have they been most scared and why?
6. When was the first time they thought they understood love and why?
7. To them, what is the meaning of life and why?
8. What about them is stopping them getting what they want and why?
9. What belief do they have that regularly creates conflict and where does it come from?
10. When was a time they were emotionally hurt?

Now think about all of those moments and write down how they may have shaped a particular worldview your character has. Has one of those events influenced how they behave day to day?

4c. Write a conversation between you and your character.

Your character is relaxing somewhere, doing whatever it is that they do. For example, they could be sitting on a park bench eating a sandwich. Imagine yourself sitting next to them and asking them questions.

It starts off banal: Why are you eating a cheese and ham sandwich? Why aren't you wearing a jacket on this cold day? Why are you here alone?

A lot will be useless, but you might find out that they eat cheese and ham because their sister used to make them that sandwich every day for lunch and they miss her, and through their behaviour you'll find they don't let anyone get close to them. Slowly among details a flaw emerges. This exercise will also get you into their voice (more in Chapter 2.1).

If you're stuck for scenarios, here are some ideas for inspiration, but think of a place they would actually be:

- Your character is on the bus reading.
- They're at the gym.
- They're working in a cafe.
- They're waiting for someone in a pub.
- They're in a hospital waiting room.
- At a house party.

Tip:
You may prefer doing this out loud, so record an audio conversation with a friend asking you questions while you take on the role of your character.

Feel free to be as expositional as possible. This is an exercise in character information, not writing craft.

Example:
Julie is in the park, sitting on a bench, looking over London.

Me: Hi
She looks at me as though I'm mad.
I smile.
Julie: Hello.
Me: What are you up to?

Julie: I'm sitting on a bench. I thought it was obvious.

Me: Sorry. I was just trying to make conversation.

Julie: Well don't. I came here for peace.

Me: Sorry…

She says nothing for a moment then huffs.

Julie: I didn't mean to…

Me: That's okay. I know random people saying hello in parks comes across as weird.

Julie: It really does. And if you say anything creepy or try it on I will punch you in the throat.

Me: Why the aggression?

Julie: Because everyone in London is awful and only talks to you if they want something.

Me: Maybe you've just met the wrong people.

Julie: No. It's in the air like a plague. Maybe it's the toxic levels of pollution, it does something to the brain and makes everyone an arsehole.

Me: Is that why you're here? Hoping for some clean, non-plague filled air?

Julie: No. My mum's moved herself into my flat and is on a cleaning frenzy so I'm spending as little time there as possible.

Me: Sounds like she's doing a nice thing.

Julie: No. She's doubling down on mothering out of guilt and so she can tell her friends, 'I looked after Julie after her heart attack. I'm a great mum!' Even though she had a big hand in causing it. She's probably forcing my step-dad to paint the walls. Chaotic, whirlwind of interference she is. Wish she'd just go.

Me: Have you asked her to?

Julie: Quite bluntly. But she does this thing where she hears what she wants to hear. My step-dad can stay, but she's given me at least ten mini heart attacks since she's been there. No wonder my real dad left her.

Me: Oh… Sorry.

Julie: I need a fucking drink.

She takes a bottle of wine from her bag and swigs it. She notices me watching.

Julie: Don't look at me in that judging way. The doctor said to reduce, not stop.

Me: No judging here. You ever thought about trying to contact your dad?

Julie: You sound like my mate, Lemar.

Me: Maybe he's right.

Julie: He's never right. And until he can sort his relationship issues out he can't tell me anything.

I nod.

Julie: I tried to contact the fucker but got nothing back. I know where he lives. I found him on Facebook but maybe my message went into that weird inbox you have to specifically look for.

Me: You could visit his home.

Julie: How many doors do you knock on uninvited? Anyway, enough of this. Have a good day. Try to avoid the plague air.

She leaves, swigging from her wine bottle.

This was tricky to write, as fundamentally Julie does not like random people so would be very hard to talk to and would not give up that level of information. However, part of her recovery is to be more positive and not shut everything down, and she finds that easier to do with a stranger than people who know her and she has established patterns of behaviour with. In this short exchange we established some useful information to go towards a flaw, and the early stages of her voice are coming through.

These exercises are designed to get you writing so you can learn about your characters in the context of an interaction.

4d. How does your character's flaw relate to their goal and how will it get in their way?

If you're stuck for what the flaw may be, have a look at the traits in the table in Chapter 2.4 for inspiration, as while some traits come from background and influences, some are informed by your character's beliefs which link to a flaw. Use the list for inspiration only, not as a substitute for scrutinising your character. The flaw needs to feel natural and create conflict with the goal. A few more examples of flaws are:

- Someone who has lost their faith
- Someone who doesn't question their faith
- Someone who can't move on
- Someone who doesn't stand up for themselves
- Someone with no self-belief
- Someone who is overprotective

My example:

As Julie's goal is to get better, her flaw is her inability to open up and show vulnerability, because that opens her up to a different kind of hurt. We learn where that comes from, which could be her father leaving her when she was younger and now seeing her step-dad, whom she adores, suffering in a relationship with her mum. So the heart, which is associated with love and life, is wounded for her. Her dad broke it and she has a negative view of love because of what she has seen from her mother. Julie also blames her mother for her father's departure, but at this stage perhaps that is self-preservation. Perhaps she is scared to admit that her father also rejected her, because it will make things worse.

So her flaw, and the thing holding her back from getting what she wants, which is to be better, is her inability to allow herself to be vulnerable, because with it comes the threat of being hurt. Her self-preservation is actually self-destructive. She also behaves in a dominant way in all relationships. They're on her terms, because dominance provides security. She doesn't want anyone's help, and until she can accept love and support she'll never be able to give it, and the heart will remain broken and in pain.

Her flaw links to the lesson she needs to learn to succeed. She is too wounded to open up, and unless she can, she will never succeed.

2
_____

PUTTING FLESH ON THE BONES

2.1. DEVELOPING VOICE AND PROJECTION

C haracter voice can be a confusing term, as some people use it to refer to a character's overall voice in the story, while others use it to define how a character sounds and speaks.

It means all of those things. Character voice is about how your character sounds, what your character is really saying, how they say it and how they project themselves. It is linked to their goal, desire and flaw, as well as their past and where they are emotionally in a scene.

Some of this may already be in your mind, as working through goals, desires and flaws naturally stirs up so much more and informs a lot of your character's voice.

A lot of pressure is put on the first words your character says and what they do, as that moment should inform the audience about what kind of character you have created. If they're the idiot of the piece, they should say something endearingly stupid like Joey in *Friends* tends to. If they're a pedant, have them be pedantic or give a disapproving look when somebody says something incorrect. If they're Carlton from *The Fresh Prince of Bel Air*, have him say something enthusiastically geeky, which highlights his self-importance. If it's Theodore Bagwell from *Prison Break*, have him exert his dominance and use typically flowery language. If they're a brilliant secret agent, show them being just that like *James Bond* films often do at the start with an intense set-piece.

Your character's voice is crucial in making them appear real and deep.

A good way to define your character's overall voice is to look at factors that influence it, which include:

1. Personality

Are they an introvert or extrovert? This will impact how they engage in conversations, whether they take the lead or sit back and wait. That could vary depending on the situation and how comfortable they feel. Whatever choices you make, remember the need to know why. Why is my character more comfortable one on one than in groups? Why is my character desperate to be the centre of attention? Why is my character obsessed with socialising?

2. Background and Experiences

Think about your character's upbringing, their friends, family, and peer groups. So much of what has gone on before shapes who we are now and our beliefs. Often these experiences are unique to us.

A lot of people construct their tastes and even the way they speak on the basis of the crowd they grew up with, as it can be common to look to outside influences for identity, thereby cherry-picking aspects from those we want to model ourselves on, from friends and family to idols. Some of those choices can stay with us. For example, I have a friend who says 'like' after every few words despite being in his late thirties. He might say, 'I, like, saw this thing, yeah, and it was, like, amazing.' That comes from how we spoke as teens in London, which in turn was influenced by TV shows and films, because that is what we were exposed to. It could also be attributed to nervousness if he is unsure of what he is saying. Alternatively, perhaps someone used to speak softly, but their dad shouted at them when they were a child, telling them to speak 'like a man,' and that now informs their tone and imbues them with some toxic masculinity they need to purge. Everything comes from somewhere, even quirks like nervous laughter, constantly humming, or saying 'umm' all the time.

Whatever point in their lives your character's story begins, there is still a lot that has gone on before that informs how they interact in the world they exist in today.

3. Culture

Whatever culture your character exists in, do they choose to engage with it or rebel against it, and why? How does the culture they have been exposed to inform their behaviour? How a character identifies with culture impacts their voice.

Religion, ethnicity, sexuality, politics and class all influence the way we speak as well. A deeply religious person, perhaps might feel uncomfortable swearing, so doesn't do that, or their religious upbringing has made them believe that you should treat people the way you want to be treated. Maybe growing up in a religious household has made them hate organised religion.

A nun might feel uncomfortable talking about sex among her fellow nuns even though she wants to explore it, so that would be in the back of her mind during conversations and may make her less interested in other matters. If you mine areas of your character's background you will find more ways to inform voice and perspective, and also what impact these things have on your character's psyche.

How does their political alignment make them feel about the world and others? Has world politics directly impacted them or a loved one, or are they protected from it? Things like class, race, and nationality are not choices made by your character from birth, they are things that they are born into, so how do they feel about themselves in relation to others?

Everything that makes up their character informs how they feel about others and themselves, so dig into these areas of your character's life. Every detail informs how people project themselves and behave in their interactions.

For example, if someone has grown up without money, they might be careful about their spending, and therefore at a dinner where their friends have consumed lots of drinks your character might not want to split the bill. Would they say something? Or would they stay quiet and pay more despite having less? That will be informed by how they desire to present themselves, based on their values, desires, and what they believe. The flip side of that might be someone who has grown up without money, knowing that the bill is being split later, consumes everything in sight to get their money's worth.

4. Physical and Outer Appearance

Just as important as our background and culture, our physicality has an impact on our perception of ourselves and the world.

Every decision has meaning. If someone wears a suit every day, why is that? Is it because they have to for their job, or do they believe that by dressing a certain way, people will perceive them how they want to be perceived? Does that person wear a suit to mask the incredible insecurity within? Do they hope outward appearance distracts from inner turmoil?

Even details like a person's height can impact how they project themselves to the world. If someone is really tall, perhaps they've been bullied and are always getting looks and jokes aimed at them, so they are quiet by nature, always nervous. Or they use their height to intimidate others.

Someone who has always been bony growing up perhaps has dented confidence, so when talking to someone they're attracted to has that issue in the back of their mind. Think about how your character perceives themselves and projects themselves, as it will impact how they behave in certain situations.

5. Worldview:

A character's worldview is influenced by their personal and cultural experiences,. Marlin in *Finding Nemo* dislikes the ocean outside of the parts he knows, because of the loss of Coral. That informs how he interacts with the world and people. He lives in fear.

Choices also contribute to worldview, and the consequences of choices that we have made can have a lasting impact on how we present ourselves to the world.

What is Subtext?

Subtext is the meaning behind what is said or done. It's what your character is saying between the lines and behind the gesture, and it is informed by emotion, so developing your character properly will allow for more powerful dialogue and interaction with the world.

It's rare a character will say exactly what they want emotionally, so it is often hidden in the subtext.

Subtext can also be secrets. In *Breaking Bad*, Walt has a huge secret that he carries into every conversation with his wife, his brother-in-law who works for the DEA, and his son. This adds tension as we know at some point that secret will be revealed and we are waiting for it.

Think about a time you've been in love but have been unable to tell that person. Every exchange you have with them is informed by your feelings. You choose your words based on the secret you hold and your internal filter.

There's a great example of subtext in *Sideways,* a film in which a struggling writer and wine enthusiast, Miles, takes his engaged friend, Jack, on a trip to wine country for a last single-guy bonding experience. Miles hopes to relax and take in the wines, while Jack is after a fling and finds one with Stephanie, while Miles connects with her friend Maya.

Later in the film, Maya asks Miles why he is obsessed with pinot noir. He explains it at length with a passion and vulnerability that hooks us in. He talks about it being a hard grape to grow, and describes it as temperamental, unlike cabernet, which can grow and thrive even in conditions of neglect, reflective of his friend, Jack. He mentions that pinot needs constant care and attention from someone patient who can truly bring out its flavours. He says that when the right person cares for pinot, it is the most brilliant thing on the planet.

He's talking about himself with someone he has been connecting with and is interested in, but he knows his faults and wants to lay them on the table in the hope she will see past them. All this comes from how he views himself and his place in the world. He's looking for the right woman who can tolerate his faults and give him the love he craves. He identifies with the difficult pinot grape but also suggests that the reward for sticking with him for long enough and nurturing him pays off with something magical.

Maya says why she loves wine, stating because it makes her think of different places and times. It evolves and gains complexities, just like her.

This is an honest scene between two characters who are a potential love interest, saying what they look for in a partner without saying directly what they look for in a partner. It's brilliant and we get to connect everything.

How much less interesting would it be if she asked him why he liked pinot, and his answer was, 'Because it's like me, hard to grow and nurture, but when you handle it properly it's rewarding?' It would also be too direct to be truthful of Miles' character based on what we've learned about him up until now. It's a big leap for him to even make this comparison and it's rewarding for the audience.

How many people struggle to tell others how they feel? It's a relatable scene and engaging from start to finish, because there is vulnerability, risk, and desire underneath every sentence.

Another example of subtext would be the well known, 'I'm fine,' when somebody is actually furious.

Subtext allows an audience to work things out and to relate to expression.

Show Don't Tell

You can also say a lot with an action. The most basic example is someone smiling or punching the air when they're pleased about something instead of just saying, 'I am happy.' It comes back to the familiar phrase, 'show don't tell.' Show what your character is feeling, don't say it.

Here are some basic examples of telling and how to turn them into showing:

In a novel:

Telling: Amir hated Lee and wanted to punch him in the face, but decided he wouldn't.

. . .

Showing: Amir gritted his teeth, clenched his fists, took deep breaths, then walked away from Lee.

By showing instead of telling, we see how the character reacts in this instance and we get to interpret actions. It's far more engaging and characterful, and how your character displays these emotions and thoughts is down to how you've crafted them. Depending on your character, rather than clench their fists they might bite the tip of their thumb, knock something over, or smile like a maniac. It depends on who they are and how they feel.

Obviously the telling example still moves the story forward, but it is boring and a lazier form of writing that keeps a character feeling two-dimensional and can disconnect an audience because the mind isn't having to do anything.

In a screenplay:

Telling:

```
INT. KITCHEN - DAY

DAN enters the dilapidated kitchen to find LARA, nervous, sat
on the counter.

                    LARA
          So how did the job interview go?

                    DAN
          It was great. They want to hire me!
          Let's crack open the wine!
```

Showing:

```
INT. KITCHEN - DAY

DAN enters the dilapidated kitchen to find LARA, nervous, sat
on the counter.

                    LARA
          So?

DAN walks over to the fridge, opens it and grabs a bottle of
wine.

He smiles at her and opens it. She leaps off the counter and
hugs him.
```

The telling example is fine, but that's all it is. The showing example offers so much more. It shows the relief between them, that they needed this and is a far more emotive exchange. The simple use of the word 'So?' carries fear, tension and a need to know. We get to read more into the showing example.

External expression is informed by so much that is internal, so give it the depth it deserves. Body language is also a part of voice, because it is about how characters project themselves, so use that to your advantage too. For example, someone is at a party and their former best friend turns up. Instead of saying 'Damn, I hate him,' show the feeling in an action. They could fold their arms, look up to the heavens, retreat into the corner to avoid them, or decide to drink everything in sight.

Knowing your character's voice will help you to determine how they behave in all situations. Also, think of your characters and how they behave in a group dynamic. If three of us are in a car and are involved in a crash that accidentally kills someone, all three of us will react differently. While there is shock, one character may be thinking about what they stand to lose, and therefore wants to drive away; another may be gripped by guilt and wants to call an ambulance; while the third may be completely devastated and unable to speak, perhaps even passing out (more on dynamics in Chapter 2.5).

How to check your character voices aren't clashing

A note you may get back from someone reading your early draft of a novel or screenplay is that all your characters sound the same. Here are techniques for prose and screen to help you to test how distinct your characters are:

For prose:

Copy a chapter with an exchange over to a new document and remove the he said, she said and names in dialogue tags. Read the dialogue aloud and see if it is different enough that you know who is speaking. If people sound the same, and I mean not just in their words but in what they want and their opinions, then you need to make changes.

For screen:

Block out the character names in the dialogue and scene actions and read the script aloud. If characters sound the same in their words and meaning, make changes to differentiate those voices further.

So when developing your character's voice. Keep in mind that:

- People are influenced and shaped by everything around them.
- How we project ourselves comes from who we are and what we want to achieve.

- People behave differently in different situations.
- Our physical appearance impacts how we feel about ourselves, and how we choose to present ourselves reveals something about us.
- There is a constant, internal narrative going on.
- External expression is influenced by internal factors and the past. Language, dialect, tone of voice, sentence structure, social interaction, and body language, all have roots in something.

EXERCISE 5

5a. Write one of the following from your character to their worst enemy:
- A letter
- An email
- A text/ messenger exchange/ group chat (this allows you to develop multiple voices)

Keep your mind on your character's personality, as it will determine how they engage in this communication. Do they dive into what they want to say, or are they forgiving, trying to bury the hatchet, or is this a hate rant?

5b. Write one of the following from your character to the person they love:
- A letter
- An email
- A text/ messenger exchange/ group chat (this allows you to develop multiple voices)

5c. Observe interactions

Next time you are on public transport or out socially, note down how people interact with each other and see if you can pick up on any meaning behind a gesture or conversation. Take notice of the nuances of speech and idiosyncrasies people have. See if you can spot any quirks someone might have. List what you assume about them based on certain things they say.

2.2. OBSTACLES

O bstacles are essential to any character journey. If a character isn't encountering obstacles, then they're not struggling and there isn't a story.

Obstacles are everywhere. For example, if I struggle to get out of bed in the morning, is that an obstacle? Yes, because I have to overcome it. Is it entertaining? Absolutely not, unless it:

1. Tests me
2. Reveals something about me as a character
3. Helps me to grow
4. Is a meaningful step towards my story goal

An obstacle should ideally be one or all four of those things.

Some obstacles are small, but the big ones force characters into difficult decisions that have consequences should they go wrong.

Obstacles can appear extrinsic, but they are only obstacles because they obstruct character, prevent them from achieving their particular story goal and are therefore important to the development of your character.

It's worth noting that the things that get in your character's way can't just be things that happen to them, but things that are consequences of their actions and decisions. They are obstacles in an active pursuit of the goal. Your character's decisions bring them face to face with obstacles.

There are obstacles that already exist in the world, for example, in a fantasy there may be a dangerous cave your character needs to enter in order to retrieve a weapon. That dangerous cave only becomes an obstacle once your character puts themselves in a position that means they have to enter and risk their own safety, and it's an obstacle because of the meaning it holds for your character. That tells us something about your character. It's an obstacle because they want what's in that cave and are willing to risk their life for it, because it relates to their story goal and their desire. To them, it's worth the danger.

Obstacles should contribute to character growth and be organic. For example, if the nun in the previous chapter wants sex but her religion forbids it, there are many organic obstacles informed by her goal, her inner conflict, and the world she exists in. If she decides to go out and meet a lover, there could be an obstacle in the form of her fellow nuns, the rules about where she lives, getting caught, and where does she even go? All of those carry consequences. The obstacles naturally emerge from her goal, her desire, and the world she exists in.

Writers often throw plot at lead characters, but plot should come from the character in a story, so by doing enough character work obstacles should flow far more easily. If an obstacle serves no purpose other than to delay the time it takes for the protagonist to resolve their problem, then it is a dud and needs to be thought about more.

Imagine a fantasy protagonist who is a young girl scared of everything. She has to navigate the dangerous forest to find a plant that can cure her dying mother. The forest could contain many obstacles that create conflict, but if nothing has changed for the protagonist from entering to leaving the forest, then there has been no true obstacle. Obstacles need to have emotional resonance within your character. In this case, they should teach the girl something about her relationship with her mother and herself, and perhaps she fails to get the herb, but learns that she can survive alone and will cherish the last moments with her mother and the memories she has.

I made a mistake in an early draft of the first book in my fantasy series *Heroes of Hastovia*. There's a part in the story where my main character has to retrieve an item from a tower. That item will help him to fulfil his story goal, so he goes to the tower but fails to get the item. That was it. A fun but worthless obstacle, because the failure taught him nothing other than that the world is difficult, which he already knew. It meant the next item he sought was far more dangerous to obtain, but in terms of his growth, this added nothing and as a result felt flat. It was plot for the sake of plot.

The fix was to look at his character. This was someone out in the wider world having lived a sheltered life, protected from the real darkness of it who has to survive. The solutions were that on this mini quest he would have to kill for the first time, and the kill would be one of his enemy's minions, making him realise that the minion is as much of a victim as himself. He would also make a choice, which causes him to fail this mission by choosing to save his friend instead of getting the item that would help him to achieve his story goal. That was a huge decision that made the obstacle worthwhile, because it revealed character, and showed him taking steps to overcoming his flaw. So, though he ultimately failed to overcome this obstacle, his worldview and view on survival changed, and he showed that he would sacrifice what he wants for the needs of others. He grew as a character, and that would go towards him being able to achieve his goal later on. The lesson is to treat obstacles as the gathering of skills to tackle the larger problem that persists throughout the story. So for our young girl scared of everything, her adventure in the forest teaches her how to survive on her own to overcome the real problem, which isn't getting a life-saving herb, but coming to terms with living without her mother.

Sometimes the lesson is unclear but other elements are still at play to justify something as an obstacle. Take *Lion*, which is based on a true story. Saroo has been living in Australia for 25 years after getting lost in India and ending up on a train that took him 1,000 miles from his home. He is obsessively trying to find his real home using Google Earth and a map on his wall. He's pinpointed so many places on the map within a radius, but he can't crack it. He finally is about to give up, and nonchalantly flicks his track pad for a while and then he looks outside of the radius and finds his home. What is the lesson here? It's hard to pinpoint. Was it that he finally relaxed? Was it that he broadened his search and his mind? It's difficult to say. He just finds his solution. However, the memories flooding back into his mind through the film help him to create the picture so that his chance discovery means something, otherwise he wouldn't have understood that moment.

It is unsatisfying to have characters overcome obstacles by luck, but this just about works, as Saroo's luck is earned through his piecing together of his history via memories of paths he'd walked, and that only comes from his obsessive search. Another thing that works in the film's favour is that we have seen an enthusiastic young boy go through something awful and lose his family, so we are hooked emotionally. We have witnessed the love he had with his family, then the despair of losing them, and having perhaps come to terms with that loss and getting on with his life, he now has hope, and hope is an awful thing if it doesn't lead to salvation.

Obstacles need to create a struggle, have consequences, reveal character, and increase the stakes. They need to show us the character within. Saroo's struggle does. The consequence is expressed as he states it, that his mother will never know what happened to him and that is heart breaking. The stakes are that he will have a huge hole in his heart, and be unable to reconcile his relationships until he finds his birth mother, which is illustrated through his romantic relationship suffering. Also, *Lion* is based on a true story so carries an extra emotional hit as we instantly place ourselves in that position.

So when thinking of obstacles keep in mind:

- What impact do they have on your character and their overall journey?
- Do they force your character to overcome something internal as well as external?
- Do the obstacles lead to character growth?
- Are the obstacles true to the character?
- Do the obstacles carry escalating stakes as the story progresses?
- What is the biggest obstacle your character could face?

EXERCISE 6

OBSTACLES

6a. List 20–30 obstacles (a mix of internal and external) that prevent your character from achieving their goal.

It sounds like a lot, and it is, but through this you'll find more of your character forms and even some of the surrounding characters grow. If you start to think of more than 30 obstacles, go wild. I often find the first few flow, then I get stuck for ages and want to give up, but then ideas for obstacles will hit you when you're in the middle of something else.

It's all about planting seeds and letting them germinate. Some obstacles will be things that happen to your character, but let yourself go and amend the results afterwards. You'll end up throwing most of them away but they're part of the process to get to the good stuff. You might even find a few days or weeks down the line that you think of better ones, but these are the stepping stones to get you closer to your desired goal, which is to write an engaging and memorable character who goes on an emotionally engaging journey.

Here is my attempt:

Julie's story goal is to get better, to beat the heart attack and the negative feelings that make her shut the world out.

Obstacle list

1. Her negative attitude

2. She hates her job, which contributes to her negative outlook, but she needs money

3. Her boss keeps hitting on her and she can't say anything as she can't risk losing her job

4. She has to leave her job to take that first step

5. Her mum, Bec, stays over because she wants to look after Julie, because she believes that Julie can't look after herself

6. Julie needs to figure out what she wants to do with her life

7. Julie has to kick Bec out, as she's making Julie's condition worse

8. Julie has to exercise more

9. Julie has to give up drinking

10. Julie has to see a therapist

11. Julie decides to put positivity into action

12. Julie decides to let go of some of her toxic friendships

13. Julie decides to date again, but struggles because she sees herself as weak and damaged

14. Julie tries to track her father down

15. Julie confronts Bec about how she treats Jim, her step-dad

16. Julie wants to help Jim to leave Bec

17. Julie realises she has feelings for her best friend, Lemar, who has a new girlfriend

18. Julie needs to tell Lemar how she feels but is scared of being hurt, and when she musters up the courage to tell him, he tells her he's engaged

19. Julie is asked to be Lemar's best man

20. Julie settles for someone awful because she's scared nobody else will love her

21. Julie is about to break up Lemar's wedding but decides to

let him go, that the best thing she can do is let him be happy with someone else

22. Julie needs to accept her dad left them, and that Bec didn't drive him away.

6b. Go through the list you've created and highlight the obstacles that relate to your character's story goal and provide the most internal growth and conflict.

Here is my attempt:

1. Her negative attitude - *More a character trait that will inform how she goes about things.*

2. She hates her job, which contributes to her negative outlook, but she needs money - *This is more of a fact.*

3. Her boss keeps hitting on her and she can't say anything as she can't risk losing her job - *This is her making a decision to stay the same and not grow. It would be something she needs to overcome.*

4. She has to leave her job to take that first step - *This will be a moment of growth for her character, as she makes the decision to be worse off financially to be better off mentally. Now, how she goes about leaving will be informed by numbers 2 and 3. We'll see her at work, hating it, being hit on, biting her tongue, so this could be a moment she explodes, or the moment when she defends a colleague against her horrible boss. The moment she leaves will reveal a lot about character, because the way she does it is unique to her, and this decision carries consequence.*

5. Her mum, Bec, stays over because she wants to look after Julie, because she believes that Julie can't look after herself - *This will lead to conflict, but isn't Julie putting anything into practice yet. It's a beat in a bigger arc.*

6. Julie needs to figure out what she wants to do with her life - *An interesting addition to feed into the bigger issue.*

7. Julie has to kick Bec out, as she's making Julie's condition worse - *Another big moment as Julie defends herself against Bec and it'll impact their relationship and how her mother reacts to her too, as from the small thoughts about her character, she isn't the sort to go quietly*

8. Julie has to exercise more

9. Julie has to give up drinking

10. Julie has to see a therapist

Depending on how her character grows, 8–10 could end up being big moments, but depend on the wider world she exists in and the relationships she has with alcohol and exercise

11. Julie decides to put positivity into action but fails - *This feels in line with a comedy due to her not having the skills to be positive, having been negative for so long.*

12. Julie decides to let go of her toxic friendships - *A step on the way to a bigger cleanse. Only useful if we get a snapshot of those friendships and see how they're all she has, otherwise it's not that hard a choice to ditch them.*

13. Julie decides to date again, but struggles because she sees herself as weak and damaged - *This is big in the sense it starts to get to the heart of Julie. She's been strong and cynical, but this new self-perceived 'weakness' of a heart attack has her showing vulnerability and change. The fact she's putting herself out there is a big thing for her to do, because rejection will hit her twice as hard due to how she feels about herself and her place in the world.*

14. Julie tries to track her father down - *This is big and comes from past trauma and I will definitely use this. Then I have to decide what happens when she does track him down. Does she realise he's horrible and it helps her to move on? Or does she get scared and run off when she sees him? Does Jim help her and then she realises he's the only dad she needs?*

15. Julie confronts Bec about how she treats Jim, her stepdad - *This is big if Bec turns on her and points out Julie's failings in* *the way she treats people. Every big moment needs to have an impact on Julie*

16. Julie wants to help Jim to leave Bec - *What is the consequence of this? How does it relate to Julie getting better? It impacts her relationship with her mum again, but how does it impact Julie's goal of getting better and her need to be vulnerable*

17. **Julie realises she has feelings for her best friend, Lemar, who has a new girlfriend**

18. **Julie needs to tell Lemar how she feels but is scared of being hurt, and when she musters up the courage to tell him, he tells her he's engaged** - *This is big because she now sees herself as able to love and open up, but is then let down by that and will now perhaps undo all of her hard work up to this point and retreat into her shell. This, in traditional story terms is when she tries to break free of her old life, but the rejection makes her want to return to it. It is a moment of loss for her and if built up to properly will have a big impact on the audience.*

19. Julie is asked to be Lemar's best man

20. **Julie settles for someone awful because she's scared nobody else will love her** - *This is her failing and realising her worst fear, because this is not her getting better. This is her falling into misery, only this time dragging someone else into it with her and accepting unhappiness.*

21. **Julie is about to break up Lemar's wedding but decides to let him go, that the best thing she can do is let him be happy with someone else** - *This may seem noble but is her failing, because she doesn't value herself enough to be with him and take that leap. If it's a romcom, she will likely have to say how she feels and not retreat into her old ways.*

22. **Julie needs to accept her dad left them, and that Bec didn't drive him away** - *Perhaps she needs to let this hurt out and accept that rejection before she can open up again. She believes her mum drove him away, when he left, and until she can accept that, she may never be able to heal her wound.*

As you can see from this I've found quite a few obstacles. It's taught me more about my character, some of the surrounding characters, and has made me sure this is going to be a romcom in the form of a film or a book.

It's a development exercise, and the point of development is that nothing is final, nothing is perfect, but it's moving forward and building character. A lot of the above will prove worthless, but it will only become worthless because it helps me to find better ideas. An issue in a lot of stories is act two, and often the reason for these acts feeling flat is because not much happens, which is really due to a lack of meaningful obstacles. By doing this exercise, you'll develop character further and find more obstacles from different areas of their life to keep their journey engaging.

2.3. MAKING HARD-TO-LIKE CHARACTERS LIKEABLE

D o we have to like your protagonist? No.
Do we have to want to spend time with them in your story? Absolutely.

How do I make my hard-to-like protagonist more engaging?

When I refer to hard-to-like characters or anti-heroes, I'm referring to characters who do not display the same characteristics as your standard hero. They don't always have a moral code in line with conventional morality, they may not be trustworthy, honest, or abide by the law.

Blake Snyder's *Save the Cat!* has now become an industry standard text when it comes to structure and its take on making characters engaging. It half-mockingly suggests you show your lead character doing something nice in the first scene we meet them, using the example of actually saving a cat. That lead character can be good or bad, and the method still works, but the idea is to create engagement instantly.

Even someone awful can do something nice, like give money to the homeless. The key to this selfless behaviour is that it has to be authentic. You can get away with having this moment of selflessness slightly later than the first time we meet your character, but the sooner the better. It isn't always natural to your story to have it instantly.

An example of an anti-hero who would be hard to connect with but who is easy to engage with through a good deed is Joe in *You*. He is a weird, violent stalker, yet early on we see him being lovely to his child neighbour, Paco, whose mum is in a relationship with an aggressive and abusive man. By giving Paco books and making this sad child smile, Joe is humanised. He goes from weird stalker man, to weird stalker man with humanity in him so we allow ourselves to stick around a while longer. It also makes sense as Joe is a bookshop manager, so is sharing a passion for something with a child who doesn't seem to have much joy at home, and due to that moment of humanity, a lot of people find a point of connection with Joe.

What the writer also cleverly does is surround Joe with worse people. While he pines for Beck, she is in toxic relationships and friendships so Joe being weird and targeting her friends and boyfriend makes Joe some kind of anti-hero to the audience as he peels away the layers of her awful life while she remains unaware.

You is a story about a bookshop manager who becomes obsessed with a wannabe writer and removes obstacles to their romance by means fair and foul

---

Joe's desire is love and we can relate to that, even though his methods are twisted. His view of the world is also expressed clearly and his goal is defined. We are seeing the world from his point of view.

It's also easy to engage with characters who go for what they want, who are active, because we aren't always actively driving the change in our own lives although we wish we could. Through stories, we get to see characters live out the consequences of their actions, which are sometimes actions we wish we could push ourselves to take.

Another character who would be difficult to connect with would be the character of Mark Zuckerberg as portrayed in *The Social Network*. He seems to struggle with empathy, but his best friend Eduardo is an everyman, who for us acts like a bridge to Mark. If a nice guy like Eduardo can like him, we can engage with his story. Also, Mark's character is doing battle in the story with overly confident, smug people who come from privilege and who exude entitlement. Mark comes across as cold and a bit mean, but when a character like that fights someone we perceive as worse, we tend to support the least hard-to-like character, who in this case is Mark. A lot of people still didn't connect with him, but there were links in place to help those who did to get to that point of connection.

Another example would be Dushane in *Top Boy* series 3. We meet him in Jamaica and he's still up to his old tricks of working in the drugs trade, but it's more to get by than to become a criminal mastermind. So why do we sympathise with him? He is working with someone who appears much worse and ruthless who lacks a moral compass. Dushane's associate kills an old shopkeeper and is about to shoot an old lady but Dushane kills him first, because he doesn't want to kill women and can see that his associate has gone too far. In that moment, although Dushane is part of a criminal world, within it, he has a moral code, and that humanises him. Dushane comes from a world where selling drugs for people in a better position is his only opportunity, yet he has a code of honour and we can respect that. Even when he is pulled back into drug dealing in London, it is to protect his own life and his disabled cousin back in Jamaica from merciless gangsters.

As far as anti-heroes go we should also look at Arthur in *Joker*. There are multiple techniques used to humanise him and to make us feel sorry for him.

- He is a carer to his mother.
- He's trying to work, but children steal his sign and then whack him in the face with it and beat him up.
- Then to make matters worse, his boss is awful to him and accuses him of stealing the sign.
- Someone Arthur sees as a friend lies and contributes to Arthur losing his job.
- Arthur is also completely cut off from society. The world he exists in, Gotham, is already divided and there is tension between the rich and the poor, yet nobody wants Arthur, because he appears strange and has a condition where in the face of stressful situations he laughs, which people interpret as weird.
- He tries to make a child laugh on the bus, but the child's mother scolds Arthur.
- His therapy sessions are cut due to funding, along with his medication.

It's hard to not feel sorry for Arthur when life keeps whacking him and he feels completely disconnected.

He is brilliantly constructed, and even when he shoots the three privileged men on the train, I was on his side. Three men were harassing a woman, then Arthur's condition took over and they pummelled him, so he shot them. He was pushed to his limit.

So from constant rejection, this is the moment things change for Arthur. He sees people take up what he did as a cause of some sort in the divided city narrative. He is accepted into something without being directly accepted.

A lack of connection to the world pushes him towards villainy. He feels disconnected from society, and later in the film, his mother. The film is wonderfully executed in how it manages to create sympathy for one of the greatest villains of our time.

So if you're writing a protagonist who will likely do bad things, or a villain, keep in mind ways to give them enough humanity to be characters that people want to spend time with. Some of the techniques are:

- The metaphorical saving of a cat - show them doing something nice early on whether that be giving someone in a less fortunate position something, defending someone etc.
- Make whoever they are in opposition to worse.
- Have us understand why they behave the way they do. If someone has always been pushed down by society or betrayed, then we can understand why they might compromise morality to get what they want.
- Have the reason they do the bad things come from a genuine position of weakness and threat.
- Save the most awful thing they do until we get to know them slightly and are engaged with them. Arthur doesn't kill anyone for quite a while in *Joker*. Joe waits until the end of the first episode of *You* before he whacks Beck's boyfriend around the head.
- In sitcom, make them get what they deserve. In *It's Always Sunny in Philadelphia* the characters tend to always lose, so we enjoy their journey of being awful and watching it all come crashing down.

Always ask yourself, do I want to spend time seeing what

happens to this character? Like all else, it is subjective, but you have the tools to increase the chances of people engaging in the story of someone who does bad things or isn't particularly sympathetic. Motivate them and humanise them.

How do I write a compelling antagonist/ villain?

A common mistake people make is not motivating their villains or giving them any depth. The most forgettable villains are bad for the sake of being bad, but the best villains have something driving them.

Jamie in *Top Boy* series 3 is completely motivated. He is young, yet parent to his two younger brothers because his parents died. Therefore, he has turned to a life of dealing drugs to support his siblings. At this point it's hard to not like him, because like Dushane, he is part of a society where drug dealing is where the money and opportunity is. Where he becomes a villain is in his methods to get what he wants. He kills pretty much anyone who gets in his way in increasingly horrifying ways. As a villain he is brilliant because he doesn't care about codes and ethics within his world. He cares about getting what he wants, and the only way Dushane can beat Jamie is by abandoning his own ethics and preying on Jamie's weakness, his brothers.

Villains always have to believe what they are doing is good. For example, Annie Wilkes in Stephen King's *Misery* believes she is doing good by forcing Paul Sheldon to write a new *Misery* novel and keeping him hostage, when in fact she is putting him through psychological torture.

EXERCISE 7

CREATING SYMPATHY IN YOUR CHARACTER

7a. Write the moment your protagonist does something nice?

Think about what motivates this moment and where this example of behaviour comes from. For example, if I'm a hardened criminal, I may stop to give a homeless person the rest of my sandwich, because I have experienced homelessness.

OR

7b. Write the moment your character shows vulnerability?

Keep in mind why they are showing vulnerability. For example, perhaps I'm leaving my secret lover's home and I am lying to my long-term partner over the phone, but I see someone crying about losing their baby and it hits me hard, because that same loss is driving the wedge between me and my partner.

Here is my example in a screenplay.
It is the second scene in my story after Julie has had her heart attack, and beneath it all, she is petrified, masking it by joking, because the truth is too hard to take.

JULIE sits up in bed. Her doctor, RANIL (42. Sick of treating fools), approaches.

                    RANIL
          So. You've had a heart attack.

                    JULIE
          Can we call it something else? Heart
          attack sounds a bit... serious.

                    RANIL
          It is serious, Julie. Someone your
          age should not be having one.

                    JULIE
          Big cough. Let's call it that.

                    RANIL
          You have atherosclerosis.

                    JULIE
          Wow, no foreplay, just straight in
          with the rough stuff.

                    RANIL
          It's a disease where your arteries
          get clogged with fatty plaque.

                    JULIE
          Plaque?

                    RANIL
          Yes, plaque. And if you want to
          avoid another heart attack--

                    JULIE
          Big cough.

                    RANIL
          Big cough... Then you need to
          reduce your stress and cut back on
          booze, cigarettes, the bad food.

                    JULIE
          Just all the fun stuff then?

                    RANIL
          I'm giving you beta-blockers to
          reduce your blood pressure, a
          statin to reduce your cholesterol,
          and Rivaroxaban. A new and improved
          blood thinner.

                    JULIE
          Surely you've not done your job
          right if I have to take all these.

RANIL ignores the comment and hands JULIE several leaflets.

                    RANIL
          Read these about the side effects.

                    JULIE
          I've just had a heart attack, the
          last thing I need is homework.

                    RANIL
          You're not to return to work for at
          least a month, and I'm recommending
          you see our consultant.

                    JULIE
          Does recommendation mean non-compulsory?

                    RANIL
          Put it this way. It benefits you if
          you want to avoid the pain you
          described to A&E as (looks at chart)
          'A bull fucking my chest.'

                    JULIE
          I've been misquoted. I said *giant* bull.

                    RANIL
          Joke as much as you want. But if
          you don't make changes to your life
          you won't make it to forty.

RANIL walks away. JULIE stares after him.

2.4. CHARACTER AND PERSONALITY TRAITS

E veryone has character and personality traits, both good and bad, however there is a difference between the two.

Character traits are influenced by morals, ethics, beliefs, values and upbringing. These are often hidden from sight.

Personality traits are behaviours and outward projections, often determined by the image someone wants others to see. These are often on display.

If I ask you what someone is like and you say they are bubbly, that is a personality trait. If you say they are honest, that is a character trait. It would also be informed by something. Perhaps the character used to work on a market stall with their mum and she placed a high value on honesty, so the character picked that trait up.

A character trait becomes a flaw when it is a weakness that prevents the character from getting what they want, informed by a past trauma or event.

Take Walter White. He is egotistical. That is a character trait, but also a flaw because he is still bitter about the past when his business partners made millions and he ended up a down-and-out chemistry teacher with cancer. His ego and pride keep him locked into his life of crime until it consumes him.

Character and personality traits shouldn't be something you clip onto a character. They should feel organic, and these could inspire flaws in your character, as when you look at why your character has particular traits, you unearth more about them. Someone isn't just born mean, that is formed through experiences, whether they experienced cruelty from their parents, or somebody bullied them daily and the only way to overcome it was to fight back.

Whether a trait is positive or negative depends on its impact on your character and how it makes them interact with the world and others.

Always remind yourself that traits come from somewhere. If someone has spent the last few years homeless, perhaps they are resourceful and cautious, as they have learned that their only way out of the situation is to do things for themselves, and maybe they were let down by someone else so find it hard to trust. Your task when choosing traits is to be able to explain where they come from.

You may find the list of traits below helpful if you ever become stuck while developing character. I'll regularly update it as I come across more. You can find it over at: www.markboutros.com/blog/character-trait-list

Adventurous	Affable	Affectionate
Ambitious	Amicable	Amusing
Analytical	Anti-social	Arrogant
Articulate	Athletic	Authoritative
Balanced	Belligerent	Benevolent
Bitchy	Blunt	Boastful
Bold	Boring	Brave
Bright	Brilliant	Calculating
Careless	Cautious	Charismatic
Charming	Chilled	Cold
Compassionate	Confident	Conscientious
Considerate	Controlled	Controlling
Courageous	Cowardly	Crafty
Creative	Cunning	Curious
Daring	Decisive	Demanding
Dependable	Desperate	Destructive
Detached	Determined	Devoted
Dictatorial	Difficult	Dignified
Diplomatic	Dishonest	Disobedient
Disruptive	Disrespectful	Educated
Efficient	Eloquent	Empathetic
Erratic	Encouraging	Energetic
Enthusiastic	Envious	Evil
Extravagant	Facetious	Fair
Faithful	Fanatical	Fearless
Firm	Focused	Foolish
Forgetful	Forgiving	Funny
Fussy	Generous	Gentle

Genuine	Gloomy	Good
Gracious	Greedy	Gregarious
Grim	Grumpy	Happy
Hard-working	Harsh	Hateful
Helpful	Heroic	Honest
Hostile	Humble	Hyper-critical
Idealistic	Idiotic	Ignorant
Imaginative	Impatient	Impartial
Impulsive	Incisive	Inconsiderate
Indecisive	Independent	Indiscreet
Inhibited	Innovative	Insecure
Insensitive	Insightful	Insincere
Insulting	Intelligent	Intense
Intolerant	Intuitive	Irrational
Irresponsible	Jealous	Judgemental
Killjoy	Kind	Lazy
Liberal	Logical	Lovable
Loving	Loyal	Mad
Malicious	Materialistic	Mature
Mean	Mechanical	Miserable
Modest	Moody	Moronic
Nagging	Narcissistic	Narrow-minded
Nasty	Naughty	Neglectful
Nervous	Nosy	Obedient
Obnoxious	Obsessive	Obstinate
Opinionated	Orderly	Outrageous
Paranoid	Passionate	Pathetic
Patient	Patronising	Peaceful
Perceptive	Persistent	Personable
Persuasive	Perverse	Pessimistic
Petty	Petulant	Picky
Pioneering	Placid	Playful

Plucky	Plodding	Pompous
Predatory	Prejudiced	Pretentious
Principled	Profound	Prudent
Puritanical	Quiet	Rash
Rational	Reflective	Relaxed
Reliable	Resentful	Reserved
Respectful	Resourceful	Responsible
Ridiculous	Rigid	Romantic
Rowdy	Rude	Ruthless
Sadistic	Sanctimonious	Secure
Scornful	Scrupulous	Secretive
Selfish	Selfless	Sentimental
Sensible	Shameless	Silly
Sincere	Shy	Skilful
Sly	Smart	Sneaky
Sociable	Sordid	Stingy
Stubborn	Stupid	Suave
Superficial	Surly	Sympathetic
Tactless	Tasteful	Tasteless
Temperamental	Tense	Thorough
Thoughtful	Thoughtless	Tolerant
Touchy	Tough	Uncharitable
Understanding	Unfriendly	Unkind
Uptight	Unrealistic	Unreliable
Unruly	Unstable	Untrusting
Vague	Vain	Vengeful
Vindictive	Vivacious	Weak
Wild	Willing	Withdrawn
Witty		

EXERCISE 8

FINDING TRAITS

8. Write an interaction between your protagonist and any other character. Make a list of what traits are on show and make a note of what influences those traits.

Here are two examples of interactions with Julie that indicate different traits through words and actions, so you can get a sense of how to highlight them, but it demonstrates that everything your character says and does has meaning and comes from something.

Example one:
I approach Julie who is sitting on a bench.
Me: Hi. Mind if I sit here?
Julie: (smiles) Sure. Great day isn't it?

Through her smiling and asking me a question we gather she is friendly, trusting and inquisitive, and has an interest in engaging in conversation.

Example two:
I approach Julie who is sitting on a bench.

Me: Hi. Mind if I sit here?

She shrugs.

Julie: Not my bench.

I sit. She shuffles to the end of the bench and buries herself in her mobile phone.

Through her words we know she isn't particularly friendly, and her actions suggest she has no interest in engaging in conversation. We gather she is <u>cold,</u> <u>dismissive</u> and perhaps <u>anti-social</u> or <u>closed-off/ untrusting</u>. Or she is preoccupied with something.

2.5. CHARACTER DYNAMICS

As well as developing your characters to be three-dimensional, you have to think about the dynamics between them. How do your characters react to each other? How do they converse with each other? How do they feel about each other? How do they get in the way of each other? How do their values clash?

We all behave differently around different people. I revert to a frustrated and impatient teenager when I'm with my parents, but with other writers I'm calm and have discussions about life and struggles as a writer. Think about how you might feel and behave differently in one group of people compared with another. Multiple character relationships allow us to reveal different aspects of our characters, and it also allows for a balanced perspective.

Characters also represent different things, as people generally have differing views on certain topics. Obviously some worldviews are held by more than one person, but nobody wants to watch or read anything where everyone holds the same set of values and worldviews. Some members of a gang or an army can share the views of their leader, but you don't want your protagonist, antagonist, and supporting cast to be approaching life the same way.

Your characters are part of a greater story and should all represent something related to it. I'll use an old but great example in *When Harry Met Sally*. The tagline is, 'Can two friends sleep together and still love each other in the morning?' Harry believes men and women can't be friends, because sex always gets in the way, while Sally believes men and women can be friends. They represent two sides of an argument.

Your characters represent different points of view. For example, sometimes your protagonist and antagonist will want the same thing, but have differing ideas on why they want that thing and see different value in it. Take fantasy as an example. A hero and a villain might want a magic orb, but have completely different plans for it. In *The Lord of the Rings*, Frodo wants to destroy the ring while Sauron wants to use it to rule.

Characters all have different intents and desires, even if it's for the same goal. If my question is, 'If you had an item that gave you one wish, what would you do with it?' Several people would have different answers. One character wants to bring their loved one back from the dead, one wants to make the world a better place, another wants to destroy the world and one wants immortality. They all want the same thing, the wish, but have different intentions for it for reasons unique to them.

In *Jaws*, Chief Brody wants to protect the town by shutting down the beach. The mayor wants to protect the town, but financially, so refuses to shut down the beach, because he wants tourism on the 4th of July, because that keeps Amity afloat. The shark, well, it just wants to eat everyone.

There's an early scene where Chief Brody is getting signs to put on the beach, warning everyone to stay off it. The mayor then talks to him and tells him there is no shark, it was probably a boat, and that everything should go back to normal. That dynamic is great, and it makes us like Brody more. He wants to do the right thing, but the powers above him won't compromise profit, and what happens? A child is eaten by the shark. It's not until Brody stands up to the mayor once his son is nearly eaten that there is progress.

On the topic of *Jaws*, another great dynamic is that between Hooper and Quint. Both believe they are experts. One through study, one through experience. Quint sees himself as a working class hero, war veteran, and he doesn't like Hooper, who is educated and opposes him in terms of what to do. Their conflict is a great source of entertainment during the battle with the shark, and they finally bond over their various injuries after they've survived a couple of attacks. From difference, comes respect.

Character and concept

I like to think of a story I'm writing as a circle and at the heart of it is my story concept. For example, say I write a story about four half-siblings who have never met until their dead father leaves them an abandoned restaurant and makes them all joint owners. Now I split that circle into chunks, each representing a character.

One of the siblings is enthusiastic and wants to get this restaurant back on its feet and in the process get to know her siblings and bond with them. She represents opportunity, family and love.

Another sibling has been struggling and sleeping rough since his marriage broke down so wants to live there, so he represents home and starting again.

The third sibling has been a failed restaurateur so sees it as an opportunity to make a success on her own and is therefore dominant and individualistic, so represents ambition.

The fourth character wants to sell it, hates the place, and hated their dad too, so represents rejection.

There you have four people with different wants and needs for the same thing, which will lead to conflict and different dynamics within the group, with each fulfilling a different role.

Conflict in opposites

A great source of conflict is opposition, so it's always good to have characters with opposing sets of values and beliefs, even if they're friends or family members. In *Sideways*, Jack and Miles want the same thing, a weekend away, but have different wants within that. One wants a fling and the other to enjoy wine. That provides great conflict internally and externally and provides moments of comedy and sadness.

Look at Will and Uncle Phil in *The Fresh Prince of Bel Air*. One is a middle-aged, rich lawyer, the other is a poor teenager from West Philadelphia who comes crashing into his world. This leads to a lot of great storylines where their differences cause conflict, but also help them to see the world from a different point of view.

Even more stark, Walter White in *Breaking Bad* is a drug lord. His brother-in-law is a DEA agent. That creates incredible tension.

Not all characters are pushing for the same goal, but if they are, give them enough points of difference to maximise conflict and bring out the best and worst in them.

So keep in mind:

- What does of each of my characters represent?
- How do their wants and desires act in opposition to each other?
- What is the major source of conflict between them?

- In what ways are they similar, and in what ways do they differ?
- What is their relationship to each other?
- Opposites attract conflict.

EXERCISE 9

9. Take two or three of your characters and place them in a scene together. This could be anything from a car crash to a dinner. Write what happens.

Remember, it isn't meant to be perfect, it's just an exercise but it will help create those dynamics and unearth more about your character. When you finish, have a look at it and analyse why they behave like this around each other. How does their dialogue and action express their differences?

Here is my example:

This scene is Julie having to tell her parents about having had a heart attack. It includes Julie, her mother, Bec, and Jim, her step-dad whom she refers to as dad, because of her unresolved issues with her absent father.

EXT. BEC AND JIM'S HOUSE - TWO DAYS LATER (11:00)

JULIE, worried, walks over a pebble-dashed driveway towards a detached house. She holds her finger over the buzzer. She presses it, closes her eyes and takes a breath.

JIM answers with a heart-warming smile.

>   JIM
>   How much do you need?

JULIE chuckles and hugs him, tighter than usual.

>   JULIE
>   I know you're joking, dad, but
>   I'll never say no to a handout.

INT. KITCHEN - DAY (11:01)

>   JIM
>   Your mum's just finishing getting
>   ready.

>   JULIE
>   OK, well... I have to tell you
>   something before I bottle it.

JIM bites his lip.

>   JULIE (CONT'D)
>   Promise me you won't over react.

>   JIM
>   It's hard to promise that. My
>   reaction is totally dependent on
>   what you say... Is it illegal?

>   JULIE
>   No, but maybe you should sit down.

JIM sits.

>   JULIE (CONT'D)
>   Now I'm totally fine. But I had...

She takes a breath.

>   JULIE (CONT'D)
>   I had a...

She points to her chest.

>   JIM
>   Breast enlargements?

>   JULIE
>   No! I had a...

She takes a leaflet and puts it on the table: 'After Your Heart Attack' with a smiling pensioner on. JULIE points to the words.

                    JULIE (CONT'D)
          That...

JIM looks at the leaflet, then at JULIE. It sinks in. JIM bursts into tears.

                    JULIE (CONT'D)
          No, no. Please dad.

                    JIM
          I can't help it.

                    JULIE
          Oh, you've got me going now.

JIM gets up and hugs her. They cry together.

                    JULIE (CONT'D)
          They inflated a little balloon in
          my artery to widen it!

BEC enters. On seeing them crying, she cries.

                    BEC
          Oh God, what's happened?

Neither JULIE nor JIM can get the words out. JULIE opens her arms for a hug. BEC rejects it.

                    BEC (CONT'D)
          You're bloody pregnant aren't you?

                    JULIE
          No... I--

                    BEC
          It's a mystery father isn't it? I
          knew this would happen. You only
          ever come over when it's bad news.

                    JULIE
          I'm not fucking pregnant!

BEC spots the leaflet. Her eyes widen. JULIE nods.

                    BEC
          Jim, no! When? How?

                    JULIE
          Mum, no--

                    BEC
          You told her before me? You two are
          always excluding me!

                    JIM
          Bec, I'm--

                    BEC
          We need to book that trip to New
          Zealand before it's too late.

                    JIM
          I haven't had a heart attack, Bec!
          I'm fine.

                    BEC
          Oh... Thank God.

                    JULIE
          Mum... It's my leaflet.

                    BEC
          Why on earth are you carrying that
          around... Oh my God my baby!

BEC hugs JULIE. Her expression turns and she pulls away.

                    BEC (CONT'D)
          You're moving back to Bournemouth.
          You clearly can't be trusted on
          your own.

                    JULIE
          What? He got New Zealand!

                    BEC
          We didn't send you to the best
          schools so you could go and have a
          bloody heart attack. All those
          opportunities.... wasted.

                    JULIE
          This is why I didn't tell you
          sooner.

BEC throws JIM the kitchen roll to wipe his face. She shakes her
head at JULIE.

                    JULIE (CONT'D)
          That leaflet says stress is a big
          factor. And if you want me to
          remain non-dead, you can't just
          launch into me.

JIM has a moment of getting it together, then looks at JULIE
and loses it again. He looks away.

                    JULIE (CONT'D)
          Why do you think I never visit?

                    BEC
Because you're lazy and always hung
over.

                    JULIE
Those are two very valid reasons.
But also, because nobody wants to
travel two hours to be told why
they're supposedly shit at life.

2.6. RESEARCH

I t's important to avoid lazy stereotypes in your characterisation. If an audience starts to smell clichés they will disconnect from your character. The best way to make characters come across as new is to do your research.

Talk to real people

If, for example, you decide to write a Lebanese character into your script, then you should talk to Lebanese people you know or friends of friends. Research the country, the cultures within it and absorb as much as you can to define that character's background and experiences. The same goes for writing about an Olympic swimmer, a student, or someone who is nervous. Talk to people who live those things and have those traits, and never solely rely on depictions in other works of fiction as they are the products of someone else's imagination. Other works of fiction are useful, but as a complement to deeper research and authenticity.

A lot of the information you find will not make the final story, but it gives you a deeper understanding of that character and helps you to avoid stereotyping. You will also create a unique voice for that character. Of course, there is creative licence to interpret and reimagine, but even that should come from a place of knowledge. We need something to reimagine and get creative with.

If you don't have a direct link to someone who may have lived what you want to research, ask on social media and most of the time somebody will have a connection and be more than willing to help.

Also, people love talking about themselves, so if you offer to buy someone a coffee to chat about their job or life, they will likely want to meet, then it's up to you to have the questions in mind that inform your character development and story.

It's always good to have pre-written questions, but allow the person to speak freely first. Learn through listening and then get the information you need if it hasn't come up. You'll be pleasantly surprised by what details emerge. If you can't meet face to face, email your questions and start a dialogue. If you're writing a detective series or something where the profession is a key element, you need to consult experts so that you are portraying a true view of that working world.

Also, in some cases people will want to maintain their anonymity, so make sure you are clear that you're conducting a research chat or fact checking and that their anonymity is protected.

What if I'm writing a historical project?

If you're writing a historical novel set in times of war, it would be important to dig into that history for accuracy. Obviously it will be trickier to find someone from that time if it took place more than a lifetime ago, so you'll have to dig through books and first hand accounts online and in your local library.

However, there is so much research you can do. Take *Chernobyl* for example. Craig Mazin read books and government reports from inside and outside the Soviet Union. He also interviewed nuclear scientists to understand how a reactor works, and spoke to former Soviet citizens to get an idea of the culture in 1986. He also read first-person accounts of people who were there to bring authenticity to the project and characters.

Go down the rabbit hole

As well as meeting people, search online for what you want to know. Some professionals and people will be hard to get a link to. For example, it will be tricky to gain access to a murderer, someone working for MI5, or an actual alien or clownfish, so do some online searches, watch any documentaries you can find on a particular subject, and read some nonfiction or listen to audiobooks.

For *The Greatest. Of All Time*, we read every book we could on Muhammad Ali, searched online for where he was in his life at the time of the incident, and we went to an exhibition that was on. We also read a lot of accounts of suicidal people who didn't go through with it so we could understand Joe more.

There may also be podcasts on what you're researching. We are so lucky to live in a time where we have access to so much, and sometimes going down the rabbit hole can even inspire stories.

The glory of research possibilities is a double-edged sword, as it also means your work will be scrutinised more heavily as people have access to more knowledge. So if you're setting something in a particular period, or portraying particular cultures, make sure you do your research to avoid bias, offence and laziness.

For example, I recently wrote a script about an accidental killing, but I obviously know nothing about this area. I could assume there would be extreme guilt, grief, and an underlying hopelessness and inability to move on for my character that would spread into all aspects of her life, but a simple online search opened my eyes to some truly moving and tragic accounts that made my character so much more genuine. It was horrible to read about, but if reading about it moved me that much and made me feel sadness and sympathy, then when translated through character it would hopefully have the same impact on an audience.

From researching accidental killings to body farms and how long it takes someone shot in the head to decompose in a basement, my search history makes for some interesting reading, but at least it makes product targeting a bit more exciting.

Whoever you are writing about, make sure you do the research so they come across as authentic as possible.

Know the difference between a stereotype and an archetype

Archetypes use a template or mould as the beginning, where you take, for example, a hero, unwilling hero, sidekick, idiot, mentor, villain etc, and build your character from there using flaws, traits, idiosyncrasies, desires, and make them unique and flip clichés. A stereotype uses a template as the end and finished product, often going over the same, tired ground without much in the way of development.

Our characters are often defined in terms of the archetype they come from. Look at Jon Snow in *Game of Thrones*, the ultimate embodiment of the reluctant hero. He's not that different from Luke Skywalker and Harry Potter in terms of being a reluctant hero, but they will all handle a situation differently based on further character development, which sets them apart.

Archetypes and stereotypes are subconscious, because they're everywhere. Naturally, we all have an image of a type of person based on our experiences, education, and whatever stimuli we've been exposed to that shapes that view. So it's up to us to make sure we're using archetypes to build from only, and that we steer clear of stereotypes. It's always good to take a moment once you've started developing a character and to think, 'What's the opposite of that?' 'What is a fresh angle on this?'

In terms of archetypes there are hundreds mentioned online, alongside debate over how many there actually are. Joseph Campbell in *The Hero With a Thousand Faces* explores the eight types of character in a hero's journey. Since then, stories have evolved and so have character types, enabled by technological advances and cultural shifts. Let your characters be who they need to be, and if they fall into an archetype that's fine. If they fall into a stereotype then change it.

If you are going to write a story about a reluctant hero, consume stories with reluctant heroes in them so you can see what you need to change to make yours unique. Ask yourself, 'How do I flip this cliché?'

Staying organised

Staying organised when you're moving between character development, research, and writing down story ideas is difficult, so here are a couple of tips:

Scrivener - Lets you keep everything in one place so you can have your research tab, character tab, and story tab. It is especially useful for those of us with a scatter-brained approach.

If you're writing a TV series or book series it is incredibly handy at helping you to stay organised. The last time I checked it cost £47 and is well worth it for the time and headache it saves you.

Google Docs - If you don't want to spend money on Scrivener,

Google Docs are free and amazing, because you can work on them anywhere without having to save and send to all your different devices. If you're on your phone you can use them when on a bus or train and make them available offline if there's no reception.

Also, we don't always write on our own, so if you are part of a writing duo or group, you can all work in the same document at the same time, so there's no hassle of having to save something and send it around before anyone else can add to it.

2.7. CHARACTER DEVELOPMENT QUESTIONNAIRE

So now you have lots of information swimming through your mind. Your character has a brain, a heart, a wounded soul, a voice, a knife and a few guns pointed at them in the form of obstacles and stakes. Now it's time to build on that skeleton, fill that history and create a fuller character, someone who has lived and breathed and interacted with the world.

One of the best scripts I ever wrote was written on a plane after completing the below questionnaire. There are hundreds of different character questionnaires on the internet. I'm not saying this is the best or that one is better than any other, but this one worked for me and I'm constantly improving it. You should use existing examples to craft one that works for you. We are all different writers. We have different processes, and the best thing we can do is absorb the experiences of others to better inform our own processes and do what works for us from a position of greater wisdom.

Normally I would have looked at a questionnaire, stopped halfway through out of boredom and stubbornly declared that I'd work it all out as I write, but on that plane I was stuck and I didn't want to watch anything, so I persisted with the questionnaire and when the time came to write, the story flowed much more easily, because I wasn't stopping as much due to having an underdeveloped character.

Half of the answers and questions never reach the final script, but having a clear image in your mind helps you to make scenes more unique. For example, if your scene is set in a car with a couple not getting on, that can feel like you've seen it all before if you haven't done enough development, whereas if you know your characters better, you can add layers to it, such as one character wanting to turn the radio up to avoid the conflict, or one constantly pulling on the seatbelt strap, which annoys the other. Things like that sound small, but they enrich character and come from you knowing more about them and what they're thinking in that moment. If a character hates conflict, then them pulling on the seatbelt strap is a manifestation of frustration and struggling to say what they feel, while another character turning the music up suggests they care more about their own peace than the needs of their partner. Character behaviour can come from the past too. If one character watched their parents split up in a car while they were in the back as a helpless child, then this entire scene would carry more meaning and they would associate this situation with negativity.

I find knowing the goal, desire, potential lesson, stakes, and understanding a bit about voice before doing this questionnaire helps, as it informs some of the answers to know the deeper emotion everything bubbles up from. Other people may find the best place to start is with the questionnaire, so do what works for you.

So, here is the questionnaire. A lot of the questions will be repeats of what you've already done, but that will help you consolidate information and scrutinise it further, even changing it. Make it your own and add your own questions if you think of any, but leave no stone unturned. Every question unlocks more of your character. You can access the questionnaire here too:

www.mark-boutros.com/blog/character-development-questionnaire

I will update it as new questions come to mind as I'm always refining it, so always check back on the site to see if there is anything new.

Also, if you're writing a robot, organisation or creature of some description, understandably, some questions won't be relevant, but shape most of the existing ones to fit whatever type of character you're developing. *Wall-E* may have been about a robot, but that robot still had a desire and goal.

Character Development Questionnaire

Basics

Character name and age. Where does their name come from? Does their name have any significance?

How do they feel being at their current age?

Gender. How do they feel about their gender and how does it shape their view of other genders?

Sexual orientation. How does it shape their worldview and feelings about other sexual orientations?

Appearance: Build, height, weight, hair colour/ style, dress sense - How do they feel about all of those things?

Do they see themselves as attractive?

How do they walk?

How do they sound?

Culture, race, politics and religion

What is their race? How does it make them feel about the world and themselves?

What is their class background? How does it make them feel about the world and themselves?

Are they religious? How do they feel about religion?

How do they feel about politics?

How do they feel about authority?

The core

What do they want more than anything and why?

What do they need more than anything and why?

What is their flaw and what experience does it come from?

What is a lesson they need to learn about themselves through the story?

What is their coping/ defence mechanism?

What do they represent in your story?

Do they believe they deserve to get what they want? Why?

Do we like them/ sympathise with them? Why?

What makes us want them to succeed/ fail?

What will happen if they fail? How will it impact their world?

What are the major decisions they have to make in pursuit of their goal?

What are the irreversible choices they make?

What are they most scared of? Why?

What are their hopes/ dreams? Why?

Family, friends, foes, home and love
What is their relationship with their parents like?

How does that make them feel?

What is their family life like?

Do they have siblings? If yes, what is their relationship with them like and how do they feel about that relationship?

Do they have any children?

Do they want children?

Where did they grow up and what do they think about it?

Where do they live now? Are they happy/ sad there?

What is their ideal living situation?

What are they like to live with?

Do they have many friends?

Who is their best friend and what makes them a best friend?

Who is their worst enemy? Why?

Who do they love/ fancy and why?

Who is the love of their life?

How many relationships have they been in?

How would they describe their first sexual experience?

What is their idea of the perfect date?

What is the worst date they've ever been on?

Have they ever been in a fight? If so, what happened?

What's the biggest argument they've ever gotten in to?

What are/ were they like at school?

Work

What do they do for a living?

How much do they earn? How does it make them feel?

Why do they do the job they do?

What do they do if they're struggling at work?

What do they want to do for a living?

What is their ambition?

How do they feel about their colleagues?

How do they feel about their boss?

What are they like to work with?

Personal

What stresses them out? Why?

What would they change about themselves? Why?

What is the biggest lie they've ever told? Why?

Three words they'd use to describe themselves? Why?

What would they say is their greatest strength? Why?

What would they say is their greatest weakness? Why?

Do they have any disabilities? How do they feel about it?

Do they have any allergies/ intolerances? How do they feel about it?

Have they ever had any major sickness or injury? How did it impact the way they view life and the world?

Do they believe they are special in any way?

How do they feel about conflict?

Is there something your character wishes they were better at? Why?

Do they have any addictions/ habits? Where do they come from?

Do they like routine or spontaneity?

Do they seek the validation of others?

What is their biggest secret?

What is their biggest regret, and why?

What makes them happy and why?

What do they do to relax?

Do they have a hobby? If yes, what is it?

Who are their idols and why?

How do they feel about animals?

Do they have any pets? If yes, how do they feel about them?

If they could be anyone, who would they choose to be?

Do they have any hidden talents?

What is their star sign? Do they care?

Do they have any phobias and are they linked to any trauma?

If they could change one thing about the world, what would it be?

Do they have a favourite quote? What is it?

Do they engage in debates on social media?

What would be the top 3 things on your character's bucket list? Is there someone they want to experience those things with?

If they could, who would they bring back from the dead and why?

If you met them for the first time, what would you think about them?

What are they like when they meet people for the first time?

Taste
What is their favourite TV show/ magazine/ form of entertainment?

What is their favourite meal?

What would be their last meal and why?

What kind of music do they like?

What is their favourite song? Is it significant?

What is the last concert/ gig they went to?

What is their favourite sport?

Key moments

What was the happiest day of their life and why?

What was the saddest day of their life and why?

What is their most treasured memory? Why?

When was a time they showed courage/ bravery?

When was a time they came face to face with their phobia?

When was a time someone showed them genuine generosity?

When did they believe they knew what love is?

What was their most memorable interaction with a random person?

When was a time they felt immense shame?

What is the one moment they would revisit and change if they could?

When was a time they were proud of themselves?

3

YOUR CHARACTER LIVES

3.1. WRITING CHARACTER DESCRIPTIONS

Now that your character is living, breathing and multi-layered, you need to introduce them.

The way that you first introduce a character is crucial and leaves a lasting image. If you're writing prose you want to excite the reader, and if you're trying to sell a script to a producer you want the character to jump off the page.

Character descriptions are hard to get right, but the internet is full of great examples for inspiration. In screenplay terms, great character descriptions make a huge difference to a potential buyer as they already start thinking of actors, while in a novel they allow the reader to create a more distinct image in their mind.

The reason people often struggle with character descriptions is not a lack of ability, but a lack of understanding of their character. Now you've been through the exercises in this book, you should understand your character well enough to be able to write a distinct description that makes them leap off the page and into the mind of whoever reads it.

In screenplays

The key in screenplays is saying as much as you can in as few words as possible.

It's important for us to know, but unless it is essential to the story, nobody cares what your character looks like in terms of things like eye colour. Casting directors won't care, and neither will a reader unless physical appearance informs something deeper and eye colour is relevant because, for example, the character was part of some kind of experiment that made their eyes turn gold. In the series *Dark*, one of the characters has a brown eye and a blue eye. The series involves a lot of time travel, so that detail actually helps us in that instance in identifying them through different time periods, and there is a more meaningful reason for the eye colours that unravels the further you get into the series.

I know we discussed the impact of physicality on how your character feels about themselves in 2.1 and its impact on voice, but that's for you to bring out in their interactions, not to go heavy on describing in your character intro.

Here is an example of basic good and bad character descriptions:

———————

DENNIS (30s, tall with dark hair, high cheekbones, wearing new white jeans and a shiny shirt, looks like he could be very aggressive but is a misunderstood and soft soul) swigs from a bottle of champagne

DENNIS (32, a gentle giant, dressed like a man you could rent) swigs from a bottle of champagne

———————

Example one is clunky. It tells us things we don't need to know in order to communicate a similar message. Nobody cares about hair colour unless it tells us something about the character within or is really unique. Nobody gives a damn about cheekbones either unless you're writing a romance and the description is from the point of view of a character that is attracted to cheekbones and pays particular attention to them.

Example two tells us Dennis is imposing but gentle and that he dresses in such a way that would suggest confidence that perhaps isn't matched by him being called gentle and swigging directly from a champagne bottle. He's either carefree, or masking a deep insecurity behind a drinking habit and party boy image, but it is far more interesting. It also allows for broader casting possibilities.

Let's write another:

A teenage girl walks towards the school gates with her head down, thinking about how rough summer has been and how rough school will be. Others stare at her so she turns the music up on her earphones. This is MAYA. She has an old uniform and an old rucksack and wishes she wasn't broke.

A girl (16) drags her feet as she walks towards the school gates. She turns the music up on her earphones, avoiding the glares of others. This is MAYA. Her shabby uniform and battered rucksack suggest she can't afford to care about her image.

The first example again is okay, but in screenplays, describing thoughts is pretty useless and the true skill of the craft is being able to imply thoughts through what characters say and do.

The second example is far more dynamic and lets us know where she is emotionally and socially.

A good technique when writing character descriptions is to make them active. Have them doing something that reveals information and creates intrigue. From this, we know Maya has a tough time at school and doesn't really want to be going there. It implies she's not so popular, and we can guess from her keeping her head down and turning the music up that something is going on. We now stick around to find out what that something is.

You can find plenty of good examples online if you search for good character descriptions in film. My personal favourite is *The Big Lebowski* and the way The Dude is introduced, so have a look at that if you get a chance.

When writing character descriptions try to write something more poetic than, 'Jason (34. Grumpy, successful, stylish)'. Write something that plants an image in the reader's mind, and if we can meet the characters while they're doing something that defines them, even better. Let the reader complete the image. If you can find that thing that sums up your character and use it as the jumping off point for a reader to fill in the blanks, then you're onto something great.

In prose

With prose, avoid boring, list-heavy descriptions, as it jars the reader out of the experience and is mundane.

You can write a list if the context is right, for example a dating app. Then it makes sense that the first time a character sees someone that they would list the features of the person they're looking at, but give it a characterful twist by adding some observations. The reason a lot of us default to a list is because it's easier and often we haven't defined our characters to the point of being able to distil something important into such a small amount of text. Keep working at it.

Here is an example of what not to do:

My dad is tall, has a big chin and is built. He has green eyes and likes to wear khakis and vests.

It won't make somebody throw your book across the room, but the reader will soon forget that description and it won't grab their attention. It would be more interesting to write:

My dad is a beast and behaves like one, and he dresses to highlight his beastliness as though he doesn't want people to see behind the beast.

This example is also in the context of the character's point of view, so this is how this person sees his dad. It's more interesting and gives an insight into their relationship. We can all visualise a beastly dad in our own way. Character descriptions in prose should progress the narrative and provide insight into character, whether it be the character describing, being described, or both.

If you're going to list facial features, place meaning in each feature. Here is an example of how to add some power to a standard list:

Pagar's face was ageless, like time had forgotten him, but in his wrinkles were experiences of joy and misery. His hair glowed like the moon and in his blue eyes was an anger unmatched even by the most violent storm.

———

That's far more visual and interesting and even sets a scene. It mentions eyes and hair but in ways that lets you in on the character that makes Pagar more intriguing.

Context and point of view

Depending on the style of your narration you may be meeting people through the eyes of your character, so the description should match their perception of that person. Why? Because it affords us an insight into your character's mind and builds more of a connection with them.

Try to introduce us to characters in a memorable way, perhaps showing them doing the thing they do, like Jack Sparrow sailing into port on a sinking ship in *Pirates of the Caribbean: Curse of the Black Pearl*. It tells us so much about him as a pirate. How often do we meet James Bond while he's in the midst of some kind of chase or escape at the start of a film? If a character is brilliant at something, show them being brilliant. Introduce your villains in memorable ways too that establish their status.

Your job is to try to make us feel something for your character right away and to build up our understanding of them. Let us into their world, their worldview, and show us what may be a problem to them.

Like all things it takes practice to get character descriptions and introductions right, but if you can arm yourself with more ways to introduce characters and make them memorable from the off, then you stand a better chance of getting noticed and making your characters stand out. Think of it like this, if we sat down and I asked you - 'Who is your character?' What would you say? You'd be unlikely to tell me about their eye colour and chin size.

So, when introducing characters, keep in mind:

- If they're in a unique world, drop us straight into it. Let us see them in action, doing what they do.
- Nobody cares about lists of characteristics unless they are relevant to that character's place in the world and the story.
- In prose, a description can be informative not only of the character, but of how the point of view character perceives someone.
- Character descriptions should work at revealing emotional place in the story.

EXERCISE 10

10a. Write a unique description for your character.

Bring them to life through their words, actions and mannerisms.

10b. Write existing character descriptions

Take some characters you love from films and TV shows and write what you think would be their character description. Write them into an action so we meet them doing something that reveals a characteristic about them.

3.2. PITFALLS OF CHARACTER

When taking your character on their journey, there are many things to watch out for that can make them slip into being forgettable or annoying.

Here are some of the pitfalls in characterisation that happen at first draft stage. By taking the time to develop characters properly these can be avoided, but if your process is to write your way through these things, then at least by knowing the pitfalls you can identify them and try to avoid them or fix them before they become too critical.

Like anything, writing is about learning and growing so we can get better at what we do, and this will help you to become a wiser writer.

Passive protagonist

As far as feedback from an editor or producer goes, this can be one of the most painful, and it means that things happen to your character rather than them doing anything. However, a lot of people don't know what it actually means at a deeper level, and I didn't for a while too.

An example would be if someone goes to the shop and the

shop gets robbed and they get shot. That is passive. Yes, they decided to go that shop, but they did nothing else. An active protagonist would go to that shop, be caught up in the robbery, but decide to do something. They would be shot or get someone shot as a consequence of trying to be brave or trying to escape, or doing whatever it is they would do in that situation. That's the key thing to keep in mind, decisions have consequences, and as long as your character keeps making decisions that have big consequences, then you will avoid the problem of passivity.

However, not all decision making is active either. For example, consider a character who is a general and is approached by a soldier who reports that there is danger approaching and that the general needs to decide whether to stay or move. If the general makes that decision, of course the decision has consequences, but it's boring. It's the general passively being made to make an either/or choice.

A more active way of doing this is writing that word has come from the general's leader that the group should stay where they are and wait until morning. That is an order from above. The general, not trusting their leader's judgement, decides in the night that she and a team of four soldiers will go and investigate further afield.

This is more active because it has the protagonist coming up with a plan, making a decision that has stronger consequences, and creating conflict. The reasons for this decision will teach us about the character as well. On top of that, the decision has the consequence of the potential loss of her life and those of her soldiers, and it could see her banished by her ruler or even hunted as a rebel or traitor. Of course, it comes from a situation she didn't plan, but now she is driving the story and not just making a choice imposed on her. She makes a new plan, and it reveals something about character.

The best way to look at it is that characters need to push forward with a plan that carries consequences. They need to be the thing that happens. They need to be the ones driving the story with their plan to navigate situations. If they want something, they pursue it and come up with ways to get it, and there is a risk in that pursuit. We get to see the successes and failures of their plan in action, and that's entertaining.

So the best way to avoid a passive protagonist is to make their goal clear and have them make a plan and make decisions relating to the pursuit of that goal.

Emotional through line doesn't make sense

The emotional through line is your character's emotional state going from scene to scene. It is the line of thought that leads from one objective to the next. If you don't know the goal and desire, that's when this can get skewed. If a character leaves one scene feeling great loss and misery, that needs to carry through into the next and inform their behaviour through the prism of their goal, at least until their emotional state changes.

We don't know enough about the character

Sometimes because we're so keen to involve our characters in an engaging story we forget to get to know them and to allow our audience to get to know them and their worldview. Small details can often create a more rounded character in the audience's minds.

It's important to bring a character's personality out in their interactions and actions. If you're writing a series, by the end of the first episode it's great to know extra snippets about a character like their favourite music, meals, views on particular topics, or for us to have heard an anecdote about their past. You don't need to tell us everything about them, but the more you can do to create a deeper character that feels real, the better. You don't want it to be to the detriment of story, but you can find ways to naturally slip that information in through action or where you set a scene. For example, how someone's flat looks can give something away about them.

Whether it's a film, series or book, I like to try to reveal a minimum of four things about my character in their opening exchanges. I differentiate them in terms of physical, personal, social, familial, societal aspects or by the hobbies and activities in which they engage.

For example, in my fantasy series, we first meet Karl visiting the graves of his dead parents, while he sips ale and eats beans. At this point he is interrupted by some builders who want to rough him up because his poor craftsmanship brought a tower tumbling down. They're about to attack him but the princess saves him.

The things we learn in one quick scene:

- Karl's parents are dead (Familial. This information let's us in on how he may feel about himself in the world).
- He has messed up every job he's tried (Societal. He doesn't know what he's good at and keeps failing so has low self esteem and feels no sense of purpose).
- He has some enemies (Also societal. He isn't even safe in a place that's meant to be his home).
- He is wasting away drinking and eating junk (Physical. Perhaps rooted in his feelings of displacement).
- He knows the princess personally and she regularly saves him (Personal).

The main character is the least interesting

Quite often, particularly in comedy spec scripts (a noncommissioned and speculative screenplay), the main character does very little while everyone around them brings chaos to their door. That can be funny but it gets tired swiftly. The best advice I ever received, and it applies to all kinds of writing, was:

Don't protect your main character

I will forever remember that. The main character is the driving force, the one you need to hammer with obstacles so that they can grow and rise and earn the success or failure of their journey, or in a comedy, keep screwing up. If characters plod along and react while everything happens around them and the surrounding characters do all the interesting things, then they won't last and engagement with them will fade rapidly.

Don't stop your main character making tough decisions, even if they are unpopular decisions. As long as they relate to the goal and are truthful, go for it. We want to see people doing things and revel in their highs and lows.

I've seen this character before

Feeling too familiar is a common problem and comes from the fact we share similar influences in terms of the films, books and television we consume and what is popular. Naturally our minds shape characters we like and those are often based on things we've seen. It's important to stop yourself every so often and ask if something is fresh or tired and put a spin on it.

Thanks to new storytelling media, you don't have to create well-trodden types. There is more potential to tell new stories than ever before with video on demand services, gaming and self-publishing, so you can be brave with character.

Sometimes I find adding a contradiction helps to boost a character. For example, the nun I mentioned in an earlier chapter. She is a servant of god, yet wants to explore her sexuality, which goes against that. You could have a prison guard who falls for an inmate. Or a world champion boxer who turns pacifist, or a secret agent who wants to get married but can't reveal their identity. Contradictions can give characters a boost of internal conflict that may set them apart from the familiar.

I don't believe they'd do that

A member of your audience might disengage with your character because they don't believe that your character would do what they just did. That comes from a lack of clarity or rushed development.

There was a huge debate around this regarding Daenerys Targaryen in the final season of *Game of Thrones,* when instead of accepting Cersei's surrender, she burns everyone in King's Landing, children included. Many people found this totally out of character and there has been a lot of debate around it, as people feel it was unmotivated, but I think it was within her character and here are some reasons why:

- Her entire upbringing was informed by revenge and betrayal, and the number one goal of surviving Targaryens is to reclaim the Iron Throne.
- Everything she has done has been with the aim of reclaiming that throne, believing it was her right to have it, yet now she and several other people know that Jon Snow has the truthful claim to the throne. The weight behind her goal has evaporated.
- Her advisors have been murdered or have betrayed

her. Ser Jorah died saving her while they protected Winterfell, a place full of people who don't care for her. Missandei was beheaded by Cersei, and Lord Varys betrayed her, while Tyrion is losing faith.

- She lost two of her dragons, essentially her children.
- The man she loves is her nephew, which weirdly is the smallest of the issues.
- During her rise to rule the Slaver Cities, it all seemed okay because she was freeing people from awful lives, but her methods of killing were as brutal as you could get. From locking people in vaults, to crucifying them. In these situations, we backed her because we saw things from her point of view, and the people she killed were bad, but we know she is capable of brutality to execute her vision of what is right.

As you can see, 'I don't believe they'd do that' is totally subjective, but we have to make every effort to make motivation clear, and perhaps with another episode or two, the writers of Game of Thrones could have further motivated Daenerys' turn or let it play out slowly. Debate is a good thing for any show, but it should never be about character motivation, or asking why a character did something.

The stakes aren't high enough

This means someone hasn't engaged with your character and doesn't care if they succeed or fail. Raise the stakes. What is the worst thing that could happen to your character? Bring them face to face with it and have its shadow lurking around every corner. Whether the threat is a person, the sale of a house, or a bomb. It needs to be present.

Also, bring the danger in early. We need to know there is a threat early. Don't leave danger out of the picture for too long and have it escalate. It needs to put increasing pressure on your character. In *Jaws*, the shark is on the scene instantly.

When it comes to pitfalls there will always be new ones to look out for, and it's worth noting your own detrimental writing habits as we all have them, but as long as you know the goal, desire, and lesson for your main character along with the stake and flaw, most clichés will be avoided. Characters are living, breathing things in our work, so let them be that.

So keep in mind:

- Does my character's motivation make sense?
- Is my character active? Are they making enough difficult, irreversible decisions?
- Is their story goal clear and do they pursue it?
- Do we know enough about them and their personality?
- Are they the most interesting character in the piece?
- Are there internal and external stakes?
- Is the threat always escalating and closing in?

3.3. CHECKLIST

Everyone loves a checklist, so check your development progress against this handy list so you are always asking these questions:

- Do I know what my character wants / what their goal is?
- What emotional desire makes them pursue that goal?
- Is that desire primal/ relatable/ understandable?
- What is the moment that forces my character to pursue their goal?
- What is at stake for them? (Internal and external)
- What will happen if they succeed at getting what they want? (Internal and external)
- What is the worst thing that can happen to them?
- What will they do when they come face to face with the worst thing that can happen?
- What do they need to learn across their journey?
- How do they change from the beginning to the end of their story?

- What are the major obstacles in the way of them getting what they want? (Internal and external)
- Does each obstacle teach them something?
- Who is their antagonist?
- How will they overcome their antagonist?

4

GET WRITING!

Now you hopefully have the questions to always have in your mind when developing character, so you don't stray down the wrong path for too long. It's natural to wander off into the woods of development, but as long as you have a rough guide of what dangers to watch out for then your characters will be better developed and you will have less work to do when redrafting.

It can be daunting trying to break our bad writing habits and keep focused on new ones, but if you put character first in everything you do, you will write better characters and better stories.

If you need more help, you can find more blog posts at www.mark-boutros.com

It all starts and ends with character.

GLOSSARY OF TERMS

H ere is a list of some of the words that have appeared in this book and their meaning.

A, B, C stories

The A story is the core dramatic story, while B is the secondary story, often the subplot and the C story is a minor story.

In some cases one character can go through all three stories, but in those cases each one represents a different aspect of their journey, so the A story could be about a job, the B about love, and the C about family.

In the case of a sitcom, the A story is the most dramatic of the three stories, the B story will be another character going through a less dramatic story, while the C story can sometimes end up being a running joke.

Antagonist

The character or characters who stand in opposition to your protagonist.

. . .

Backstory

Your character's history and background, a lot of which informs their forward motion and is the reason they are the way they are today.

Beat

A beat is a dramatic action that contributes to a scene.

Character Arc

The transformation of a character over the course of a story.

Character Archetype

A typical example of a person or thing that should be used to build upon.

Desire

The emotional desire, relatable and understandable, they believe will be fulfilled by the goal being achieved - the approval of a parent, the adoration of others, acceptance, survival.

Flaw

A deeper emotional wound in the character that impacts their chances of achieving their goal. Their flaw constantly threatens their progress and makes them want to return to their normal state and not change. It is an imperfection, a belief or bias. It is something that keeps them rooted in their current state. In *Star Wars*, Luke doesn't believe in himself or trust the force.

Genre

A category based on the similarities shared by particular stories. Examples would be horror, comedy, romance, action, biopic etc.

Goal/ Story goal

The character's goal in the story. It is what they are pursuing - the magic lamp, the Olympic medal, the destruction of a ring, the prize money to keep the gym open.

Logline

One or two sentences that sum up the core conflict of the story. Core conflict refers to the struggle between protagonist and antagonist that communicates what is at stake as well.

Primal need

A basic human need that is universal, such as the need for survival, shelter, love, money, security, connection, identity etc. These are relatable. Even if we haven't had these threatened, we understand them, and understanding is the key to empathy and connection.

Protagonist

The leading character in your story. The one driving the action.

. . .

Show Don't Tell

The act of revealing information through action instead of telling us that information. It is important to know when to show and when to tell, as telling is not a bad thing. In a book I would much rather be told a character took a taxi from their home to a party than see them leaving home, ordering a taxi, waiting for the taxi, getting in, sitting in it, then arriving at their destination. Unless it is of dramatic importance or revealing of character, there is no need to include it.

Stakes

The consequences of failure, which would mean the character's world falling apart. The bigger the better.

Stereotype

A fixed idea of a particular type of person.

Tagline

This is the line on the poster, the attention grabber, the line used to sell the story to the audience. For example:

Alien - In space, no one can hear you scream.

Jaws - You'll never go in the water again.

The Big Lebowski - Her life was in their hands. Now her toe is in the mail.

ACKNOWLEDGMENTS

This has been a tricky book to write, as for every argument there is a counter argument and I've nearly given up on it several times, wondering if anything in here is of any use. What should have taken one month has taken four, but I think it's worth it and if this book helps one person, I have succeeded. If it helps hundreds, I can buy new shoes.

I want to thank my editor, Jasmin Naim, as she gave me that extra push to refine the material, get more references to back up my points, and helped me to turn this into something far more useful than I could have imagined.

My appreciation also goes out to Bobby Birchall at Bobby&Co. He is a brilliant cover designer and he was very patient with me changing my title, and his expertise took a terrible concept I gave him and turned it into the cover you see.

I also want to thank my creative writing tutors. At the time of learning I was useless and probably didn't show my appreciation, but 90% of the good to happen in my career is because of what they taught me.

An old friend of mine in both senses of the word, Patrick Mahon, also has my eternal gratitude. We have spent hundreds of hours chatting about writing and battling through story struggles, and a lot of what I have seen and read is down to him. When it comes to screenplays he has always set the standard for what I hope to write.

Thank you to you, the reader. I would've never written this if it wasn't for the encouragement of people over on my blog. You make me believe I have something worthwhile to share, even if you are just saying it to be nice.

A special thanks also goes to Adam Croft, who not only is a brilliant author, but an excellent mentor. His advice when writing this book was invaluable and the fact he gave up his time to read it and answer my questions will always be appreciated. His knowledge of everything to do with writing is inspiring and makes me want to keep improving. When I was in full imposter mode his patience and kindness went a long way. If anyone is interested in getting into the world of the independent author, then you should have a look at his courses at indieauthormind-set.com. His crime thrillers are also brilliant.

My biggest thanks of all goes to my wife, Cinthia. She works in a completely different industry yet finds the patience to listen to me talk about this stuff as though it is a real job. Her encouragement and belief has a greater impact on me than she will ever know.

You are all excellent.

REFERENCES

Films:

500 Days of Summer (2009) Directed by Marc Webb. Written by Scott Neustadter and Michael H. Webber. Dune Entertainment

Alien (1979) Directed by Ridley Scott. Written by Dan O'Bannon. 20th Century Fox, Brandywine Productions

Amelie (2001) Directed by Jean-Pierre Jeunet. Written by Guillaume Laurant. Canal+, France 3 Cinema, UGC, UGC Fox Distribution

Avengers: Infinity War (2018) Directed by Anthony Russo and Joe Russo. Written by Christopher Markus and Stephen McFeely. Marvel Studios

Ex Machina (2014) Written and Directed by Alex Garland. Film4, DNA Films

Finding Nemo (2003) Directed by Andre Stanton. Written by Bob

Peterson, David Reynolds, and Andrew Stanton. Walt Disney Pictures and Pixar Animation Studios

James Bond: Spectre (2015) Directed by Sam Mendes. Written by John Logan, Neal Purvis, Robert Wade, and Jez Butterworth. Columbia Pictures, Eon Productions, Danjaq LLC, and Metro-Goldwyn-Meyer

Jaws (1975) Directed by Steven Spielberg. Written by Peter Benchley and Carl Gottlieb. Universal Pictures

Joker (2019) Directed by Todd Phillips. Written by Todd Phillips and Scott Silver. Warner Bros. Pictures, DC Films, Born Studios, Village Roadshow Pictures

Lion (2016) Directed by Garth Davis. Written by Luke Davies. The Weinstein Company, Screen Australia, See-Saw Films, Aquarius Films, Sunstar Entertainment, Cross City

Pirates of the Caribbean: The Curse of the Black Pearl (2003) Directed by Gore Verbinski. Written by Ted Elliott and Terry Rossio. Walt Disney Pictures and Jerry Bruckheimer Films

Rocky (1976) Directed by John G. Avildsen. Written by Sylvester Stallone. Metro Goldwyn Meyer

Sideways (2004) Directed by Alexander Payne. Written by Alexander Payne and Jim Taylor. Michael London Productions

Star Wars: Episode IV - A New Hope (1977) Written and Directed by George Lucas. Lucasfilm

Taken (2008) Directed by Pierre Morel. Written by Luck Besson and Robert Mark Kamen. EuropaCorp, M6 Films, Grive Productions, Canal+, TPS Star, M6

The Big Lebowski (1998) Written and Directed by the Coen Brothers. Working Title Films

The Social Network (2010) Directed by David Fincher. Written by Aaron Sorkin. Columbia Pictures, Relativity Media, Scott Rudin Productions, Michael De Luca Productions, Trigger Street Productions

Wall-E (2008) Directed by Andrew Stanton. Written by Andrew Stanton and Pete Docter. Walt Disney Pictures, Pixar Animation Studios

When Harry Met Sally (1989) Directed by Rob Reiner. Written by Nora Ephron. Castle Rock Entertainment, Nelson Entertainment

---

TV Shows:

Breaking Bad (2008 - 2013) AMC

Chernobyl (2019) HBO, Sky Atlantic

Curb Your Enthusiasm (2000) HBO

Dark (2017) Netflix

Fleabag (2016-2019) BBC

Frasier (1993 - 2004) NBC

Friends (1994 - 2004) NBC

    Friends. The One With All The Rugby. Season 4 Episode 15 (1994-2004) NBC. 26th February 1998

    Friends. The One With The Birth Mother. Season10 Episode 9 (1994-2004) NBC. 8th January 2004

Game of Thrones (2011-2019) HBO

It's Always Sunny in Philadelphia (2005) FX

Parks and Recreation (2009 - 2015) NBC

Prison Break (2005-2009. 2017) Fox

Seinfeld (1989 - 1998) NBC

The Amazing World of Gumball (2011) Cartoon Network

The Dumping Ground (2013) CBBC

The Fresh Prince of Bel Air (1990-1996) NBC

The Greatest. Of All Time (2017) Sky Arts

The Office (2001-2003) BBC

The Reluctant Landord (2018 - 2019) Sky One

Top Boy Series 3 (2019) Netflix

You (2018) Lifetime

Books:

Boutros, Mark. (2017) *Heroes of Hastovia Book 1: The First Adventure.* Mark Boutros

Campbell, Joseph. (1949) *The Hero With A Thousand Faces.* New World Library

Goldman, William. (1973) *The Princess Bride.* Harcourt Brace Jovanovich

King, Stephen. (1987) *Misery.* Viking

Rowling, J.K. (1997) *Harry Potter and the Philosopher's Stone.* Bloomsbury Publishing PLC

Shakespeare, William. (2002 edition) *Macbeth.* Simon and Schuster

Snyder, Blake. (2005) *Save the Cat.* Michael Wiese Productions

Tolkien, J. R. R. (1949) *The Lord of the Rings: The Fellowship of the Ring.* Pantheon Books

THANK YOU

Thank you for reading.
I hope this book has been useful and assists you in getting to
where you want to be.

I post regular blogs on my website: www.mark-
boutros.com/blog.

You can also contact me there if you want to hire me for story
development, script editing, or any other writing related tasks.

If you found the book useful, please leave a review, and you can
contact me via the website if you want to discuss anything
further.

Printed in Great Britain
by Amazon

10889378R00099